# *All My Georgias*

# Redjeb Jordania

# *All My Georgias*
### *Paris — NewYork — Tbilisi*

*The Official Seal of the Democratic Republic of Georgia: St George over Mount Kasbek with the seven heavenly bodies of antiquity symbolizing Georgia's seven provinces.*

An earlier version of this book saw light for the first time in a Georgian translation from the original French. It was published by the Friedrich Ebert Foundation in Tbilisi, 2004, with a reprint in 2011.

A short English language preview appeared as part of a collection in Icarus No. 6 (NY 2001). Also, some chapters are included as discrete stories in the author's publication *Escape from the South Fork and Other Stories*, Driftwood Press, NY 2009 (Amazon.com).

# Acknowledgments

Many people encouraged me in the writing of this book. Above all I would like to thank Peggy Backman for her support and painstaking help with the editing, and Dominic Ambrose for his translation from French to English of most of Part I, *Growing up in Leuville*.

\*\*\*\*\*\*\*\*\*\*\*\*\*\*\*\*\*\*\*\*\*\* .

# TABLE OF CONTENTS

FOREWORD

INTRODUCTION: From Presidency to Exile
*by Professor Stephen Jones*

## PART ONE:
## GROWING UP IN LEUVILLE

# PART TWO:
# TBILISI, AT LONG LAST

# Foreword

In September 1990 the long-awaited occasion to go to Georgia for the very first time of my long life came to pass. As the son of Noé Jordania, president of independent Georgia at the end of World War One, it had been unthinkable to obtain a visa for the Soviet Union even after the death of Stalin, who considered my father, a social-democrat, as one of his greatest personal enemies: a country's memory is very long, and half a century is nothing for a bureaucracy! But with *Glasnost* and *Perestroika*, with the fall of the Berlin Wall just a few months before in November 1989, things got better, the Soviet paranoia abated, and a voyage to the Soviet Union became possible even for those who had been excluded.

I found myself in Tbilisi just in time to witness some of the events which would lead to Georgia's proclamation of independence and the election of Zviad Gamsakhurdia as president ... and his fall, just-about a year later.

But for me even more important was the simple fact of finding myself physically in the real Georgia, to breathe its flagrances, to rub shoulders with its people, and quite unexpectedly confront some of my childhood's inner demons that I did not know still lurked in my conscience.

This first encounter with the land of my ancestors is what made this book of memoirs psychologically possible. My cousins and relatives from Tbilisi and Lanchkhouti as well as many historians, students and other Georgians showed an avid interest in the life in exile of their first president, my father Noé Jordania, the Georgian colony in Paris, and of course the chateau and cemetery in Leuville, near Paris, which to this day remains the main center of the Georgian diaspora. Their questions forced many events and memories to the surface of my consciousness, and thus, without perceptible effort, they found a new life on paper through the magic of writing.

I hope this memoir adds a human dimension to the historical figure of President Noé Jordania, the father of modern Georgia, as well as my mother Ina Koreneva, other historical figures, and in general to the history of the Georgian colony in exile in Paris and Leuville.

And I dedicate this book to my children, nephews, nieces, and all their descendants, wherever they may be, so that with its help they'll never forget their roots in Georgia.

---

# Introduction

By Professor Stephen Jones, Ph.D.

In March 1921, President Jordania and members of his government boarded an Italian ship in the Georgian port of Batumi. They were bound for Istanbul, fleeing the Red Army invasion which ended the brief life of the Georgian Democratic Republic. They were forced to abandon not only an innovative experiment in democratic socialism but their homes and in many cases their families. None returned to Georgia, except to Soviet prison or execution. They spent the rest of their lives in exile, most of them in France. Noé's wife, Ina Koreneva, was pregnant when she boarded the ship, and Redjeb was born in Paris nine months later in December 1921.

Redjeb Jordania has written a fascinating memoir of his childhood and youth among the exiled Georgian community in Paris. It is a personal story, but also a plea for memory. It begins with Redjeb's visit to his father's village of Lanshkhuti in Guria in 1990, just before the collapse of the USSR. There was then almost nothing left in this village – now a town – to remind Georgians that this was the birthplace of their first democratically elected President. The Soviet authorities erased every memory of the Jordanias – the house, the estate, and the family graves including that of little Andreika Jordania, Redjeb's elder brother, who died at the age of twelve.

Curiously, after 12 years of independence and adoption of the first republic's flag, there is no public monument to that republic or to President Noé Jordania, an innovative theoretician, a national leader, and a statesman. Noé Jordania awaits his proper place in history even in his own homeland.

Redjeb Jordania's memoir is humorous and well written. Redjeb was an aspiring musician and writes delightful vignettes of his teachers Nicolas Stein and Monsieur Becker.

One of the most amusing passages describes his delirious music lesson amidst the British bombardment of Paris. But the memoir is also an important record of the lives of Georgia's politicians after they left power, and in particular of Redjeb's father, Noé Jordania, who died in January 1953, two months before that of his Bolshevik rival and fellow Georgian, Josef Stalin. In the last decade, we have learned much more about the Georgian Democratic Republic from Georgian historians, but Noé Jordania is still an enigma, under-researched and his works underappreciated. Redjeb Jordania provides personal insight into the character of his father and to his no less intriguing mother, one of the first women to study at the Sorbonne's Faculty of Law.

In old age, Noé Jordania undoubtedly changed, but his charisma, his qualities of leadership and self-discipline are apparent in his son's telling. Redjeb describes his father's library, his reading tastes, his circle of friends, his view of religion and patriotism and his dealings with agents of the communist Georgian government. He introduces us to some of the great figures of Georgian social democracy and European socialism – Akaki Chkhenkeli, Evgenii Gegetchkori and Konstantin Kandelaki among them. He recalls his parents' lives in their previous exile before the 1917 revolution among revolutionaries like Lenin and Trotsky.

The Jordanias, like their fellow exiles, suffered great privation. Redjeb tells us his father never bought a new suit in his entire 32 years in exile. These sorts of things, of course, did not matter to these Georgian humanists who had suffered worse under tsarism. But their life in the "Chateau" in Leuville just outside Paris, out of the maelstrom and forgotten by the international community, must have been a hard blow for these activists to bear. They continued to work for Georgian independence but after the League of Nations recognized the USSR as a legitimate state in 1933, the Georgian government in exile, led by Noé Jordania, lost its official status. Nevertheless Noé Jordania and the Georgians in exile never ceased working and fighting for the liberation of Georgia from the Soviet Union.

In the final section Redjeb Jordania describes his first visit to Georgia in 1990 amidst the excitement and anxieties surrounding the election of the former dissident, Zviad Gamsakhurdia, as head of the new non-communist government. The context was similar to that of the first republic – imperial collapse, domestic conflict and massive economic decline. Redjeb shares his diary with us which has some fascinating insights on the new leaders.

This little book is a personal memoir. It is naturally selective and episodic, but it touches on many of the major issues and characters that have shaped the life of the Georgian Republic and its people. It adds color and important details to Georgia's long-suffering story in the twentieth century.

*Professor of Russian and Eurasian Studies at Mount Holyoke College, Stephen Jones is the author of "Socialism in Georgian Colors: The European Road to Social Democracy, 1883-1917" (Harvard University Press, 2005); "War and Revolution in the Caucasus: Georgia Ablaze" [ed.] (Routledge, March, 2010); "A History of Independent Georgia, 1991-2010" ( I.B. Tauris, 2012).*

---

# Part One:

# Growing up in Leuville

# 1. Closing the Circle

**Lanshkhuti, Republic of Georgia, November 1990**
They stood to the side. In a semi-circle. Talking in whispers. Respecting my silence. Respecting my retreat into the tumultuous memories summoned by the stone jutting out of the fading grass. "The circle has been completed... seventy years already... But the circle has been, finally, completed..." A circle without a beginning, although it had clearly reached its end. A circle closed upon itself, holding me the man, me the child, whole at long last within myself.

"They tried to erase all traces of your family," I had been told many times. "*They*" were the Georgian communists, those Makharadze, Orjonikidze, Stalin, who seven long decades ago had helped organize the Red Army invasion, the conquest of their own country by the Russian Soviet forces. "Your father's house was here," pointing to a grassy lot where a pair of long-haired black piglets were scurrying, hunting for chestnuts. "They even demolished your grandfather's and your brother's graves," that brother I never knew, but whose ghost overshadowed my whole childhood. "All that remains is this corner of a headstone stubbornly sticking out of the ground. And they didn't think to chop down the magnolia your father planted. There it is, regal now, behind the flower stand."

That autumn Sunday the village of Lanshkhuti was almost deserted. The local soccer team was playing in Tbilisi, the capital, in what was the most important match of the season; and all the locals, led by the town dignitaries, had set out to support their heroes. No mayor, prefect, police chief, party secretary. I was relieved: there would be no solemn ceremonies, no official banquet lasting for hours, no long—winded hypocritical speeches, as generally happened whenever I was recognized. We had done well not to announce our visit. Undoubtedly the first visit in seventy years of the son of the late Georgian President to his father's village would not have failed to spur an overwhelming program of celebrations. Georgian hospitality is not known for moderation: for them, too much is not enough!

It was precisely to avoid this that we had arrived unannounced from Batumi. "We" included my childhood friend Thina, with whom I had been raised in Paris, and whom I had not seen for some 45 years. She had settled in Batumi, a nearby seaside resort. With her came several relatives and friends, since no one does anything alone here; and from Tbilisi, especially for that occasion, had come my relatives Tsira and Marina Gugushvili, together with Leo Jordania, and his wife. Leo was one of Lanshkhuti's most famous sons: at a young age he had become a celebrated soccer player, member of the Georgian national team. Now, *that* is fame!

All told, ten people considered it their honor and duty to escort me for what was ostensibly my first encounter with the paternal village. They did not realize that of still greater significance for me was confronting the memory of my older brother Andreika. He had died at the age of twelve, before I was born, yet in some way created me, since he wanted a little brother to be named Redjeb, after a great—grandfather of that name whose character and adventurous life he greatly admired.

My father and his friends had often spoken to me about Lanshkhuti, which represented the center of their lives, the locus of their childhood. The details escape me, after so many years, but the impression remained that it was a small village surrounded by fields, where among others lived a whole clan of Jordanias divided into some twenty families, descendants of a common ancestor who had settled there in the 18th century. I remember a certain knoll that the locals had dubbed "Jordania hill", also known as "the Hillock of Thought". There the men gathered towards dusk to solve the world's problems and share the local news, while the women, in the kitchens, ground walnuts and corn before cooking the evening meal. It is unlikely that these Jordanias were industrious. Nature is generous in Georgia, and little effort is required to harvest its riches. My mother, who was Russian, often told me how, when she first came to Lanshkhuti, she could not but ask, after a few days: "But where are the peasants?", since she never saw anyone working the fields.

I thus had the impression that Lanshkhuti was but a small village. What a surprise to discover that it was rather a small town, which its inhabitants had ironically but affectionately nicknamed "little Paris." There were fields, all right, but far away, on the outskirts. And my ancestral home—or rather ancestral lot, since the house no longer exists — is located right in the center of town, on the main street, next to City Hall.

*1990: the ancestral site*

The house, which I know only through photographs, was typical of the Guria province, where winters are mild and snowfalls scarce and far-between. It was a one-story wooden house, adorned with a covered porch, standing on a stone platform, and had no basement. One can see houses like that in the villages, still inhabited, but now with electricity and running water. And some unique exemplars have been preserved in ethnographic museums with all the housekeeping details of an extinct lifestyle. Now that communism is a thing of the past, — we hope for ever—, the city fathers are contemplating establishing a museum in honor of my father and locating it in a replica of the demolished house on its original site.

I find it curious that although the communists demolished house and grave, inexplicably they left the lot vacant, erecting nothing more substantial than a small flower stand. They even left undisturbed the grove of trees and the magnolia that my father supposedly planted — an anecdote that seems to me rather apocryphal. True, a tea factory built in the thirties extends onto the property, but only minimally. I also find it interesting that despite their hatred for the Jordanias and the Mensheviks in general, the Bolsheviks allowed my grandmother Cristiné to live and die in that same house. When my parents were forced into exile in 1921, they wanted to take her with them, but she refused: "I well know that if I don't go with you I'll lose my son and my grandchildren, whom I may probably never see again. But if I do go, I'll lose my home, my village, my country, my reason for being..." She thus stayed on, and lived six more years until 1927 without being harassed in any way; it was only after her death that the Bolsheviks destroyed both house and gravesite. It makes one think that in those times even they had a sense of decency.

My grandmother was not buried in the garden, since that was no longer allowed, but in a small cemetery in town. The cemetery was later demolished and replaced by a park with a children's playground. As for my grandmother's remains, no one knows what became of them.

Thus it was that in November 1990 I stood before the remnants of the grave, in what had been the garden of my father's house, now an untended lot where a grove of slender trees reaches to the sky, including that famous magnolia supposedly planted by my father, in front of which romantically stands a flower kiosk. Nothing marked the spot, except for what appeared to be the corner of an ordinary stone sticking out of the short grass.

"This is actually the tombstone underneath which Andreika and Nikoloz have been put to rest," Leo explained. "We always knew it, but no one ever dared mark the spot in any way or do anything about it. You have no idea what a handicap it was to be a Jordania. It was difficult or impossible to find work, and many Jordanias were deported to Siberia, never to be heard of again. Children in school were taunted by their comrades, and you know how hard this type of thing is for children. Myself, if I had been born earlier, I never could have become a national team soccer player. It is only because Stalin had died, and de-Stalinization took place, with the profound change of attitudes that went with it, that I could succeed. Before that time, my name would have kept me down, as it did many."

Yes, it was for me a trying moment to find myself for the first time in my ancestral village in front of the grave of that twelve years old boy who for all eternity will remain the big brother I never knew. He got hurt while playing "giant's steps," a game that consisted of a sort of carrousel revolving high overhead around a central pole, and long straps. Children would hang on these straps, running in circles, and when momentum was created, would take giant steps, touching ground only at wide intervals. My brother fell, got a concussion, meningitis followed and, given the state of medicine in those times, died.

What a tragedy to die so young! For him, for my parents, and also for me, even though I was not yet born... When I was a child, I hated Andreika. I hated him because his presence in our house was overwhelming. There was a painting of him on his deathbed hanging over my father's bed. There was a sculpture of him dominating the salon, downstairs. And my mother was always telling me how good he was, for ever holding him up to me as an example: everything he did was

7

admirable, and I was made to feel totally worthless in comparison. Poor Andreika! He was only a small boy when he died, he never did anything to me. Yet there it was...

I thought I had long ago exorcised these childish emotions, but there must have been something remaining, since they came surging back with such force. My whole childhood flooded my mind in an instantaneous surge, all my family stories suddenly surfaced. The edge of time past rejoined the present to become a single entity: The circle had been closed! Yes, the circle was, at long last, complete! The physical circl, that brought my flesh back to the place from which it had sprung; and the emotional chasm that had so long remained between my brother and me, the unknowing, was finally bridged.

Yes, that circle too was at last completed. Yes, finally I could see Andreika as the small boy he had been, carefree, enjoying life, that small boy who used to tell our parents: "If I ever get a little brother, I want him to be called Redjeb." And indeed I was born, and my name is Redjeb, and I am now seventy years old and I am standing on the spot where the flesh of my flesh returned to the earth that nurtured it for so many generations.

I stood deep in thought for I don't know how long; stepped towards the kiosk; selected an armful of flowers—Leo rushed forward in order that I not pay — and laid them on the mossy edge of that stone that nothing distinguished from any other. I meditated for a few more moments: no, I wouldn't let myself be overcome here, in front of everybody; no, with a great effort, I bound my childhood memories in a mental shield and put them aside for later. And I returned to this life, to the friends, the relatives who were waiting there for me, and we continued on our way, the air of Lanshkhuti sweet to my soul...

————————

*2007: The ancestral site with reconstituted tombstones for my grandfather Nicoloz, Grandmother Cristiné, and brother Andreika*

# 2. Childhood
**Fleeting images**

## Birth

My very first childhood memory is a false one. I know perfectly well that it is composed of visual images superimposed onto oft-repeated accounts. I can see it, oh, so clearly: an apartment with somber drapes and heavy furniture, and a great canopy bed where my mother brought me into this world, Avenue de Versailles, in Paris. I can see the building's façade and the window through which I enter, bizarrely, just as I enter the world. I see my big sister Nini – three years older and so much bigger than me! – peing into a flower vase. Why didn't she have access to the toilet where there was a chamber pot? Undoubtedly because outside of that room with its drawn curtains where she remained, possibly with my other sister Atia who was seventeen years old at the time, beyond that room was unfolding a mystery which neither one of them was allowed to witness: my birth.

I see myself naked, red and yellow, issuing from my mother's womb, which I can't see at all. Completely yellow, because at the first contact with the world that had expected me for nine months, I caught a violent case of jaundice! Yes, to this day our world with its beauties, vices, horrors, with its poetry, mysteries, absurdity, with its traps, rules, seriousness, this world has nothing to offer that can make me think that the newborn I was could have been wrong. The jaundice went away, of course, but its causes keep assailing us from all sides, at every moment, inside of us as well as from outside.

## Rabbits; and a dog named Lord

And then, I find myself in a rabbits' cage. How good it smelled of dry straw and moist fur! How nice and cozy surrounded by these little lives that sustained me without ever demanding anything in return! I don't see myself enter, no, I am already there, a small, eternal moment. I see the iron mesh, the wooden latch pivoting on an old nail driven into the worm-eaten door which itself hangs off of leather hinges. On one side is a white rabbit, its quivering nose poking at a bunch of cabbage leaves on top of which lies a carrot. On the other side, a beige rabbit, undoubtedly a mother surrounded by little bunnies half her size. These are a bit frightened, climbing one atop the other, trying to get as far away as possible from the giant monster that I must represent to them. And then, nothing. No follow up. The tableau simply fades away, disappears, as though I have closed the photo album. But the feeling of warm security remains with me, will remain in me for a long time.

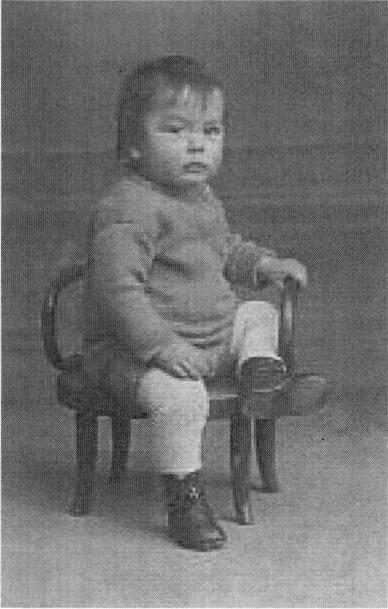

It must be years later that I see myself in Lord's dog-house. He is Namo and Valodia Gogouadze's big dog. Even though Lord had become my special friend, he did not like it at all that I should steal his home, so he would grab me by my jacket collar in order to pull me out while I clung onto the inside. And while he was pulling, and growling, and attempting to get in with me, I held on and wouldn't let him do it. This game went on over a long period of time, until I became either too old or too sensible, alas! to devote myself to it wholeheartedly....

**The Quince tree**

We are all perched on the branches of the quince tree in the deepest part of our garden in Parc Saint Maur, a remote suburb of Paris, which we would soon leave to live in Vanves.

*Childhood*

Of course, despite all the warnings against it, I bit fully into the green fruit to immediately spit it all out. Disgusting! The quince is a respectable fruit when cooked in compote, but it is so bitter when raw!

In any case, that day we were sitting in the highest branches; me, my sister Nini, Ninouka, Tamara Tsouladze and I don't know who else. I was at the most five years old. The girls were much older than me, the eldest, Tamara, was nearly nine! But in spite of the age difference, it was I, the boy, that was seated highest. On the other side of the wall, in another garden, there were three or four children of the French family that lived there. We, from our high perch, began to brag:

- What does your father do?
- My father is President, I said proudly.
- That's right, Ninouka backed me up.

And then Nini, generously:
- Well, their father is a state minister.
- Oh la la. And my father is a doctor.
- A President is greater than a doctor.
- If you're sick, a doctor is greater than a President, no?
- Yes, but we're not sick.
- Well, my mother is a schoolteacher.
- And mine makes clothes for fashionable women, said Tamara.

Indeed Madame Tsouladze kept her household going all her life with her fashion atelier, first at La Motte Piquet and then near l' Etoile, rue Lauriston.

- I won a prize in French, said the boy facing us. You want to see?
- Oh, yes.

13

And all of us admired the beautiful volume bound in red with gilded edges and borders.
- What's your prize called?
- Le Corsaire Rouge.
- Have you read it?
- Not yet, but it's really great!

Not wanting to be outdone, I said:
- I don't go to school yet, but I can almost read.
- Either you can or you can't, said the girl.

Nini came to my rescue:
- In any case, our father is President...

And that's it, the scene stops there, nothing more. The house in Parc Saint Maur doesn't leave me with any memories whatsoever. My only remembrance is of a small tricycle, all rusty and abandoned in the bushes of the park. How small and dirty it looked! Yet at the same time I knew that I had sat astride it when it looked nice at some earlier time already nearly forgotten, when it had been shiny, new and much bigger, it seemed, since at that time it had been just my size.

**Behinds**

Another early memory comes back to me. We are all very young. I don't think I was more than five years old. The smell of hay in the sunshine, the freshness of sheets in the semi-dark afternoon behind closed shutters, made all the sweeter by the stifling Sun, King of Summers, outside. It was one of those summer holidays that my mother took us on, perhaps to the Vosges Mountains that year? In any case we had the use of an entire farm, with cows, horses, poultry and farm produce all around us. Oh, how I loved to pretend I was leading the livestock to the stable at nightfall, with the dog Bouvier with the large black spots on his body and on one eye, who believed it his duty to keep the cows moving forward by biting the tips of their tails while making an awful grimace, since he didn't really like doing it.

## Childhood

It was the time when there was an ironclad belief that young children should take a nap after lunch, so my mother sent us into the bedrooms with the shutters closed; me, my sister, Ninuka and her sister Tamara, Claude, and other rascals. And all these little animals spread out, sprawling in a tangle as soon as the parents' backs were turned... often awaking suddenly, surprised to have slept. We took to playing a game that sent us into paroxysms of giggles, so loud that an adult would often come to check on us, wiggly but close-mouthed.

The game consisted of sniffing each other's behinds.... well, not just that, there was a whole ritual that I can't quite recall, but the sniffing of asses was the culmination. How long this game went on, I couldn't say, perhaps the length of one summer? After that it disappeared without ever coming back. And we never spoke about it again.

Many years later I had the occasion of meeting one of my little friends, who gave herself airs of a distinguished lady. She was then nearly 60 years old. Tired of her pretensions and stuffiness, I whispered in her ear, "Stop putting on airs, remember when we used to sniff behinds?" Oh what a shock!

## The Inkwell

I can still see the teacher, moon-faced, sallow complexion, mousy-brown hair combed back, his tortoiseshell glasses hanging askew over one ear, black ink streaking down over his face, tie, long gray smock.

This was in elementary school in Vanves, near Paris. I was in first grade, so I must have been only six years old, and must have misbehaved or refused to obey — which does not surprise me because this is a trait that I still have to this day: a visceral rejection of authority, wherever it comes from, even if it is to my detriment.

At that time corporal punishment was still allowed in schools, it seems, and to revisit this episode, I guess my chubby teacher, confronted with my stubborn refusal to obey, had grabbed me under his arm and spanked me despite my struggles.

The poor man! I was only six years old, but I was not about to put up with such a treatment. As soon as he put me back on my feet I grabbed an open inkwell — at that time each desk had one — and with all my strength smashed it in his face.

And this, vivid, is the picture that sticks in my memory: the teacher in his long gray smock, flabbergasted, dripping ink all over his face, his smock, even his shoes.

And that's all. No follow-up. I guess I was taken out of that class, or perhaps it was he who was transferred or fired. My next memory finds myself in another class with a different teacher, thin, bearded, energetic. I remember him as strict and stern, but fair: in his class I never had the slightest difficulty.

We must believe that my reputation spread everywhere, because after this episode, no one touched me ever again.

**In the Colony**

The major holidays of my childhood were the 26 of May (Georgian Independence Day) and Georgian Christmas. On these occasions the whole colony would come together, without regard to disputes, differences of opinion or political arguments, which characterized the rest of the year. In spite of these manifestations of discord, which were at times very sharp, deep down inside all the Georgians remained loyal to each other.

The great meetings and parties took place either at the reception hall of the Sociétés Savantes, or later, in the halls of the Foreign Legion, where we gained access thanks to the participation of certain Georgians in the Legion where they conducted themselves in an exemplary fashion. So well, in fact, that to this day one of the regiments of the Legion is still called "The regiment of the Georgian princes".

Of course, we children were all put on display, and time was always set aside for us to get up in front of everybody, one after the other, and show off our little talents. Dance a *Lecouri* or a *Mtioulouri*, play an instrument – usually the piano, or recite a Georgian poem. I still remember:

*Patara Khartveli var.....*

And *Tchito tchito tchiorao, rao batono melao?*

Later, when I was an adolescent, it was up to me to play the piano so that everyone could dance the Georgian dances— more or less well, but with lots of ardor and spirit. I was flattered by the attention that I received, given that I was the only young person able to bang out those dances on the piano. But at the same time I regretted that I couldn't dance like everyone else, in order to integrate myself more into the group, instead of being somewhat set apart because of this responsibility.

From that period I recall some anecdotes: A certain Georgian, arriving in Paris, announces that he has noticed that nearly all the houses were owned by just three large landowners, who must therefore, be extremely wealthy. In fact, at that time, the buildings had signs above the entry saying: "Water, Gas, Electricity", in order to show that they had been modernized. And those Georgians thought that these were the names of the owners!

And also this little story about a Georgian who buys some plums, finds a worm in the first, the second, the third one, and thinking that this is a special French delicacy, waits for nighttime to eat the rest of them, so as not to see what he is swallowing. And also, this saying, that we repeated over and over in a sing song, a Franco-Russian-Georgian saying:

*Chto takoy? Qu'est-ce que c'est?*

*Mochka kochka oukouce*

*Mochka kochka patrice*

*Vot gamovida chto takoi qu'est-ce que c'est?*

It didn't make any sense at all, and it still doesn't make any sense, but it always made us burst with laughter... just like those absurd phrases that were making the rounds in France during that period: *"C'est vot'fils, Madame? Quel oeuf!"*

17

(Is that your son, madame? What an egg!) Or, *"On n'est pas des boeufs!"* (We're not cattle!), phrases that people uttered to one another, in reference to nothing at all.

Besides Christmas and the 26th of May, we Georgian children often met on Sundays on the occasion of birthdays, baptisms, marriages or simple afternoon teas or parties at the home of this one or that. On rare occasions we would go to the movies and even rarer to the theater or to concerts. I believe that the first time I attended a concert was at the age of twelve. The opera came even later. As for us coming together after school in the afternoons or in the evening, it was out of the question. First of all, our homework took up our time, and also we lived too far from each other to be able to visit each other just like that for a short while.

**The *Chévardéni***

The colony established a sports club, the *Chévardéni*, and anyone of us, big or small, could belong by paying a modest sum to cover expenses. Of course, from the moment that we were old enough to take the bus and metro alone, we all became members, all of us young people, because besides the sports activities, this was an opportunity for us to meet often.

In winter we gathered in a gym on Avenue d'Orléans, on Tuesday evenings, if I remember correctly, from 7:30 to 10 P.M. The main sport was basketball. We formed several teams: adults, small children, young men and young women, and we practiced one against the other. At times, we played matches against corresponding teams from other organizations.

During the warmer seasons we would meet on Sunday afternoons or on Thursday afternoons in the stadium at Porte de Versailles, or later, on the playing fields at Issy-les-Moulinaux. Yes, we could meet on Thursdays, because at that time there wasn't any school on Thursday. Instead we had school on Saturdays. People worked six days per week, including Saturday –the French were envious of what they called *la semaine anglaise* — the English week —, because it was said that in England it was customary to work mornings only on Saturdays.

The adults served as volunteer instructors, at least those that knew something about sports. Besides coaching our basketball games, they also had us practice gymnastics: we learned horizontal bar, the high jump and the long jump, the parallel bars, the rings, and others. For us schoolchildren this constituted a supplement to the sports and gymnastics that were compulsory in high school. At the *Chévardéni* it was different. First of all, this was a choice, and not an obligation, and secondly, instead of being a bit lost in the midst of an undifferentiated mass of students, we found ourselves together, warmly embraced by the security of the tribe that the Georgian colony in Paris represented for us.

The gyms and stadiums chosen for the *Chévardéni* were located in the southern part of Paris and its suburbs, undoubtedly because the majority of the Georgians lived in the fourteenth and fifteenth arrondissements, or at Malakoff, Clamart, Meudon, Issy, all in that part of town. At any rate, it was very convenient for me, as I lived in the same area, in Vanves. Leuville, site of the Georgian chateau, was also in the southern part. Perhaps that area was chosen for the same reason of proximity? It makes one believe that tropism was in full effect.

When wartime came, the *Chévardéni* disappeared. We young people, now of college age, continued to meet, of course, particularly because there was a renewal of interest in learning Georgian dances. We met once a week for the courses given by a man named Petriashvili and also by Shota Abachidze – both of them "prisoners" liberated by the Germans.

As for the Chévardéni, it was reconstituted during the 1950s, but I don't know how long it lasted after that.

# 3. The Eternal Family

## Our Household

I can't say that I have a first memory of my father, my mother, my sisters or the other people around me. As far as I could tell, they were eternal, since they had no more of a beginning than my little mind attributed to my own self.

Oh, even as a child I knew that I had been born, that therefore, there was a time "before", but like all children, I didn't have a clear idea of it. Nevertheless, unlike many who apparently ask the question, "where was I before I was born?" I don't remember ever having asked, nor to have ever even thought about that absurd question. Yes, people spoke to me about "the time before you were born", but this meant nothing to me. And now that I am nearly 70 years old, this still means nothing to me.

Certainly, there is truth in that time "before", chronologically speaking, but at the same time my "before" is nothing more than a myth without anything concrete to support it. "Before" can only exist in my conscious mind, and that is filled with that evanescent present, so dear to philosophers and quantum theorists. And if anyone tries to convince me by citing books, recordings, paintings, monuments, geological ages or the universe… all of that only exists in my living self, in your living self, in the you that are reading my words, if you actually exist.

So it is not at all surprising that I don't have a first memory of my parents. My father just *was*, eternal. Big and standing tall, with blue eyes and a white beard, and a cane in his hand, he remained himself throughout all the years, except for a certain stooping over after the age of 80. At home, in the winter he wore his legendary shawl about his shoulders, in the folds of which, at the dinner table, he liked to hide one of the kittens that in long succession shared our home with us. Right in the middle of the evening meal, which traditionally was served at 7:30, with we four seated at the table—my parents, my sister Nathela and I — that kitten would suddenly poke its head out, climb onto the shoulder of my father — who didn't notice anything, we were convinced, — stretch out a nimble paw and try to snatch a morsel from the laden fork, as it traveled en route to my father's mouth. He would act totally surprised, and I would rejoice for that mischievous kitten that was capable of surprising such an imposing man!

**Father's Days**

Yes, we were four at the table, everyday, afternoons and evenings, because my father was always home, and my sister Nathela and I returned from school for lunch, as everyone did in that period, except for those unfortunates who ate lunch in the cafeteria because both of their parents worked (My other sister Atia, 17 years older, had her own place). In spite of that example, which seemed to me so distant, it never entered my mind that my father might not always be there.

His habits were regular: rise at 8 A.M., at which time he would come downstairs from his room to find his own breakfast tray of tea, biscuits and butter, which he would take back up to his office. He worked, wrote, and read until 11 A.M. Then he would come down for his morning walk, which he accomplished with a brisk pace and energetic step. He was so punctual that the neighbors and merchants set their watches by his passage. At noon he was back with a loaf of bread or other grocery items. Then, lunch, which lasted, possibly, a half-hour. At one o'clock he went back up to his room for a nap, after which he worked again until five o'clock, at which time he took another walk.

22

Often, almost every day, someone came to pay him a visit and accompany him through the streets of Vanves. But these were Georgians much younger than he was, since his own contemporaries couldn't keep his pace, so fast did he go! These others came around six o'clock to discuss politics, plan projects or just to chat and, in good weather, to play *Nardi* – backgammon -, on the balcony. Dinner at 7:30, for which one or more visitors might remain, and at nine in the evening he would return to his room, where he read before going to sleep. That was practically every day, except when we went to the country at Leuville, or when we had a *Keipi*, or banquet, at the house, which was rather frequently before the war, as I remember.

**The Importance of Democracy**

It wasn't until a long time later that I understood to what extent education and democracy were important in the eyes of my parents. For me, child and adolescent, they were eternal givens, like I was myself, me and my surroundings, like the world, the planets, the universe itself which in certain cosmogonies will most certainly have an end fore-ordained by entropy, and yet have no beginning. But for my parents, and especially for Noé, to live in a country where all the children went to school, where all the men were able to vote (at that time women still didn't have the right to vote in France), where the newspapers could print whatever they pleased about the highest personages and express the most brutally opposing opinions without the government throwing the journalists in prison, all that was for them a daily marvel.

The reality was that for them, during their childhood, in the country where they grew up, lived, suffered, nothing of the kind existed. And it was simply to attain those rights which for me and all the French people seemed to be a natural part of the social fabric, that my parents had worked and struggled all their lives, only to be finally vanquished by the armed forces of an expanding communism, and to be obliged to flee into exile, that exile where I was born, where I grew up, where they lived for more than thirty years, and which never ceased to be exile.

## The Right to Vote

My father had received a special residency card from the French government that gave him the right to vote in France, even though he remained all his life a "Refugee of Georgian Origin", which is to say, stateless, since the League of Nations recognized the USSR in 1933 "in its borders" and thus *de facto* its brutal conquest of Georgia. And he never failed to vote. Each time was for him a solemn day. He never lectured me about it, but I understood very well, even as a child, that he was going to perform an action with a transcendental significance. What's more, he was quite proud that he, a foreigner, had been considered worthy enough to participate in the political life of France, to help choose the elected leaders in whose hands the destiny of this foreign people would be put into question, again and again. It was not the election results that seemed important to him, at that point – and considering the quality of most of the elected officials of the 1930s, that was certainly not surprising – but the simple fact of participating in democracy in action. He never failed to exercise that duty and privilege that was the right to vote, except, of course, during the war years when the little honesty that remained had been shamelessly betrayed.

## Noé, Humanist

I will leave to the historians the task of formulating their ever changing hypotheses concerning the political figure of Noé Jordania, and his role in his time and in Georgian history. This is a personal memoir, with all the errors, weaknesses and false memories that all writings of this genre never fail to contain. Yet, these so-called defects paradoxically render these memories more accurate than the meticulous research that historians and biographers indulge in with the purpose of better approaching their subjects. I don't need to approach my subject, I am my subject. By this I don't mean to say that I am writing about myself from fifty years ago, that the "me" from that time is the subject. Not in the least. If that were the case, I would be compelled to use the same methodology as that of an external biographer. I am the subject because the me of fifty years ago and the me that is writing are all one indivisible entity.

The *me-persona* that is writing is at the same time, author and subject at the time of writing, even when writing about long ago events with faulty memories and interpretations. Just like an object of art, for example: it doesn't exist in itself, per se, but is always located someplace in between the observer and the object in question. So it is with autobiography, which concerns itself with events that are located somewhere between the writer at the moment of writing and the events in question. This phenomenon plays out even when the events are heavily colored by emotions. The emotions are always in the present, or else they are no longer emotions. Either one experiences the emotion again in all its fullness, or nearly, at the moment of recalling it to memory; or the emotion becomes a separate "event" by dint of time, distance, experience and all the possible "noises", as the communication specialists have named everything that might impede clear transmission.

However, in order to be able to write about distant personal events, one must distance oneself somehow while at the same time fully feel again that which one is attempting to reconstitute on paper. Thus, it is impossible to re-create a scene from one's childhood, for example, as seen from a child's point of view. All attempts at this genre can be nothing more than poetry. If there is any truth in the present work, it is to be found simply in the text itself, including the interventions of the me-author at the exact moment of writing. Therefore, my reflections on my father, my family, my life in that mythic and distant time are neither more nor less accurate and valid as any historical reconstruction could ever aspire to be.

Of course, as a child, and for a long time after that, I never stopped to consider who that unknown personality, my father, really was. Even today, I couldn't elaborate with any certainty. He appears clearly only within the complex cultural milieu in which he evolved and which influenced him so strongly. One important component of his personality could be defined as the "honest man" of classical times, so dear to the French and to westerners in general; literate, politicized, humanist, and somewhat elitist, since the phenomenon that Ortega Y Gasset baptized as "the revolt of the masses" hadn't as yet taken place, or at least hadn't as yet claimed its place center-stage.

Raised to maturity in the tsarist Georgia of the late Nineteenth Century, my father couldn't help but look at the western world from a different and critical perspective. He saw the bourgeois west as containing numerous deplorable aspects. For example, he often referred to the inner nobility of the Georgians, both country folk and princes, that he contrasted favorably with the commercialized, petit-bourgeois crassness of western countries. He noted the place of honor that women occupied in Georgian society in all social strata – remember that this is a nineteenth century man talking – compared to their situation among the Russian people and in European society. Regarding France, he noted in particular the decadence of politeness and of male attitudes:

"I remember forty years ago, when I was in Paris," he wrote in 1933, "every time that a woman entered, the men got to their feet and offered her their seats. And that is in conformity with the nature of the sexes. Women cannot stay standing as long as men can. But that is forgotten, nowadays. In the ten years that I have been in Paris, I can safely say that I have never seen a man offer his place to a woman, not even to an elderly one."

What would he have said if he had lived to see the shameful way so many women are treated in present day Georgia? Far from being chivalrous, the Georgian men take advantage of their physical strength and their egocentric attitudes to push in front of the women at every occasion, and where women are relegated to the most tiresome work.

For example, waiting in line at the bread shop, the only male among about twenty women, I was able to witness how some men enter, go directly to the counter, jostling those already there, if necessary, demand to be served and obtain that service despite whatever protests, the employees also being women, of course! Similarly, when the doors open to enter an airplane or a train, since there are no reserved seats, there is a mad rush, and all the men run to get ahead of the women and children to get the best places – without any shame. What's more, I very rarely saw anyone offer his place to a woman, even elderly and loaded down with packages.

My father wrote in his memoirs: in Georgia women never work in the fields. Well, in Kakhétie, for example, it is women that work in the vineyards and harvest the grapes. I can see them, their faces lined with wrinkles, their clothes in tatters, their ankle boots pierced by holes and worn down at the heels and so formless that the women could walk only with difficulty. In the group that I remember so clearly, they all looked to be 70 years old or more, but by their youthful gestures and movements, I am sure that they were no more than 35 or 40 years old.

It's the same at home, where it is naturally the women who do all the household chores, even when they work fulltime, just like their husbands. And at a *Supra*, one of those dinners that seem to go on forever, it is naturally the women that are in the kitchen while the men lounge at the table. Once in awhile, the *Tamada*, or toast-giver, will make a great speech in honor of the women, who are asked to come to the table to hear themselves thus honored. As Lala told me: "And we stand there, forced by custom to listen to our praises, while we are wondering what is burning in the kitchen and thinking that it would be a lot more appreciated if the men lifted a finger to help us, instead of all these empty words...."

But getting back to the topic: In spite of all his criticisms, my father highly appreciated the achievements of western thought, and he never tired of discovering the new worlds it offered. His favorite occupation was reading the great authors: poetry, philosophy, novels, history, political economics. It was in his library that I became acquainted with Michelet, Balzac, Adam Smith, Auguste Comte, Victor Hugo – whose *The Art of Being a Grandfather* became his bedside reading at the birth of his first granddaughter, Ethery Pagava — and also the Greek and Roman classics, which he held to a very special veneration.

I don't believe that I have ever heard anyone refer as often as he did to Aristotle, Thucydides, Herodotus, Marcus Aurelius and Gallienus, among others, and with such familiarity that he might have had them as personal friends.

He also possessed in his library a beautiful bound edition of the works of Karl Marx, which included volume after volume of correspondence between Marx and Engels. Was it the books beautiful appearance, all gilded, that attracted me? Or the fact that they were usually under lock and key? In any case more than once I managed to borrow one of those volumes on the sly and peruse it without understanding a thing, to then put it back discreetly in its place. Was it for that reason that when I became of the age to interest myself in such things that I found myself incapable of reading Marx.

When the weather was nice, on Sundays, my father often took his morning promenade among the bookstalls on the banks of the Seine, where he rarely missed the opportunity to bring me some book that he judged to be at the right level for my understanding. Jules Verne, Fennimore Cooper, Dickens, Alexandre Dumas, Jack London, Paul d'Ivoi are among the authors that colored my childhood. At times – and what a treat! – he took me along with him, but then I never knew which book to have him buy for me; how to decide among all those treasures?

Something that I didn't understand for a long time was that my father was the embodiment of a synthesis of social revolutionary, Georgian patriot and learned European with lofty ideals, supremely conscious of the intrinsic value of the human being, whatever the degradation in which the person might have fallen. "No one falls down so low that there isn't still in him something worthy of being saved," he said, rejoining the notion of Christ the Redeemer.

He had always been agnostic, it seemed to me, and he hardly believed in any organized church, but he recognized in religion a very important function in the life of a society. And even though he didn't go to mass, he made it his duty to attend all the great religious feasts, such as that of Saint Nino, who brought Christianity to Georgia during the Third Century, and all the funerals, marriages and baptisms of all his compatriots.

## Religion and Me

As for me and religion, my parents left me completely free, so free that they never spoke to me about it. In fact, I don't remember ever hearing anyone speak about these questions, and this is in spite of the fact that the father of my mother had been a village priest. Naturally, I never heard any talk of religion at school, which in France is resolutely secular, and never among my playmates. Yet, I don't know how or why, but at the age of 13 I decided to become baptized! This was solemnly done at a small orthodox Russian church in Vanves, the Georgian colony not having at that time a place of worship of its own.

I remember having chosen as my godfather Doctor Tsintsadze, a family friend who practiced in Africa, with the simplistic idea that he would invite me to come visit the Dark

Continent about which I had read so much! That never happened, though; my parents never let me go because I was too young for such an expedition, and then when I was old enough, the war began. In any case, once the baptism ceremony was done with, I never once went into any church to simply go to church, but only on the occasion of some social ceremony, such as a marriage or a funeral, and of course, for grand concerts, such as J. S. Bach's *Passions* or *Oratorios*.

But even with all this, I did not remain totally ignorant, because an old friend of the family, Madame Rousseau, took responsibility for my religious education, albeit in her own singular way: "You learn all about the Greek and Roman myths at school, and the Egyptian ones, too. Well, I will now teach you about the Christian myths." And I must say that seen under that aspect, western Judeo-Christianity does not lack interest.

It remains that to this day, and although I had wanted to be baptized, I do not understand the need that humanity has to believe in the divine. In fact, I believe that the greatest failure of communists was not political, economic or social, but rather, religious: they had 70 years in which to eradicate religion, and in spite of all their efforts they weren't the least bit successful, just the opposite.

**President in Exile**

The role of President of a government in exile is highly ungratifying, especially if the situation extends not just over a period of years, but decades. After the invasion of Georgia by the Soviet armed forces in 1921, the Georgians, like the Russian émigrés, waited for the Great Powers to intervene and for the Bolshevik regime to quickly collapse. Thus, they considered their exile to be temporary: there were numerous examples of noble émigrés who, having brought with them small fortunes in jewels or other liquid assets, went about spending recklessly, without a thought to the future, so convinced were they that their possessions would soon be returned to them, only to eventually find themselves reduced to the most abject poverty.

That certainly was not the case of the great majority of Georgians, who had not left behind any great assets, especially the members of the Social Democratic Party, led by my father. Upon arrival in Paris in March 1921, President Jordania and his associates were received officially by the French government as the legitimate representatives of Georgia. They opened a Georgian Legation on Rue la Boétie, which became the official seat of the Georgian government, continued to enjoy the *de jure* recognition of the great powers, and began to engage in intense political activity at the League of Nations and with the Great Powers for the purpose of liberating Georgia from the Soviet yoke.

The years passed. The first great blow to their hopes: France and the other countries recognize the USSR, albeit with explicit reservations in the case of Georgia, the annexation of which was not recognized. Then, some years later, the second great blow: the League of Nations recognizes the USSR within its borders, including Georgia. The immediate consequence was that the Georgian government in exile lost its official status, the Georgian Legation was obliged to close its doors, and Noé Jordania became a simple civilian – except in the eyes of the Georgian exiles, who always considered him their president, even his political enemies who often attacked him vigorously.

The reason was that they were united in their hate for Bolshevism and for the colonial status imposed on their homeland after the tsarist appropriation of 1803. Georgians belonged to a great number of political parties, which never ceased to quarrel with great enthusiasm. One can really say that when three Georgians get together, they make up seven political parties! And not only among the exiles: we have seen this clearly in Georgia itself after 1990, where, with the dawn of a new political freedom, more than 160 parties were created, and where one could say that the Georgians of the homeland assumed the fratricidal fighting of the émigrés, but this time with cannon fire, since now they had the means.

Although he became a private citizen in 1933, my father continued to officially represent anti-Communist Georgia and as such, to have a certain amount of access and influence through the backdoor among the western governments, with France at the head of the list. Thus the Georgians, both friends and enemies, often came to him to ask for his help whenever they needed him to put in a favorable word with the authorities. My father received all of them, because he made a strict distinction between his duties as President of all the Georgians on the one hand, and those as leader of a political party on the other. He never closed the door on any compatriot, and he made a point of not showing favoritism, except of course when it was a matter of political issues, in which he remained true to his own principles for his entire life.

However, one doesn't become the head of a government without an iron will and well-proven steadfastness. My father, with his outward appearance as a serene patriarch, well knew when to display these qualities when he considered it necessary. As, for example, in the case of Kako Nijaradze

## Kako

He was a man about 40 years old, stocky, not too tall, somewhat porcine in appearance, who arrived in Paris toward the end of the war. I don't remember anymore if he was one of those Georgian soldiers who, having been taken prisoner by the Germans, had been liberated because they had family in France — his father had been an old émigré who lived in Leuville, near Paris. Or whether, and this seems to me to be more probable, he arrived after the liberation. In any case, it became quite clear that he was a KGB agent. He inserted himself in all the Georgian social circles, gathering information about everyone, and propagandizing with fervor, pressuring everyone to return to Georgia and thus weaken the anti-Communist cause. Since the great majority of the exiles still had family in the USSR, he certainly had means to pressure people. Informing, lies, threats, blackmail were for him, all legitimate means and he was successful in that a certain number of his compatriots let themselves be trapped... until one fine day, after having undoubtedly displeased his superiors, or having fallen himself under suspicion, the KGB gave him his orders to return to Tbilisi.

I was at home when he came, terrorized, to ask for my father's help in getting France to accord him asylum. For two hours he spoke, he begged, he described the horrors that awaited him, to which he had not hesitated to send so many others. He repented, proclaimed his regrets, his contrition, admitting to all his deceptions, his tricks and his crimes against Georgia and the Georgian people.

I can still see him crawling on his knees, even actually kissing my father's shoes, all while crying out in his panic and despair. "Help me, I beg you! Help me to stay in France, help me to escape... you know how cruel and ruthless they can be over there. They will torture me, for days, for months! They will treat me like an animal, at best they will send me to end my days in the atrocious conditions of the Siberian gulag...."

And my father, stone-faced and impassive, looked at him and listened to him. When he was exhausted, Kako finally stopped, prostrate before my father, who then bid him farewell. I never heard him mentioned again.

*Growing up in Leuville*

# 4. Maternal Affairs

The business of everyday life was, of course, my mother's affair. What a ruthlessly energetic woman! She was always up by 6 A.M., and she never went to bed until late at night, in contrast to my father, who enjoyed some ten hours of sleep every night, plus an after lunch nap. While he was susceptible to chills, and always wore a shawl on his shoulders except in summer, my mother was always too warm and only wore the lightest clothes, even in winter. She attributed this to the state of her heart, which was fragile and for which she took valerian drops.

These were popular in the medical practice of the time, and I can still vividly smell the distinctive odor. In fact, in her old age, she survived several heart attacks. The last one, when she was over 80 years old, was so severe that the doctors gave up hope. But she made a complete recovery to the astonishment of all. Whenever someone proclaimed it a miracle, she would explain, "There was nothing miraculous about it. I quite simply found my condition revolting. It was in the middle of all that pain when I decided: to suffer in order to live, that is acceptable. But to suffer in order to die, that is totally idiotic. So I survived."

As for my parents' conjugal relations, these were either nonexistent or well hidden from my sister and me. In any case I have no remembrance of ever having seen them in the same bed, much less in more intimate circumstances. My father's bedroom was very clearly his and his alone, with a large double bed and a night table in which, as was the custom at that time, was hidden a magnificent chamber pot. My mother, on the other hand, spent the few hours that she dedicated to sleep on a daybed in a small room on the ground floor where she also kept her sewing machine and her iron. However, I never had the impression that that room was truly her own. In certain regards, the three of us, my mother, my sister and I, were nothing more than appendages of my father, so dominant was his presence in that house, which he practically never left.

My mother's state of health never seemed to slow down the rhythm of her activities. She was always ready to do everything and anything for the family, the émigrés, the homeland, the Cause. She kept herself up to date on all the international political events and right up until her death at 90 years of age she was passionately interested in the evolution of morals and ideas in the world. At that time we had very little money to go with our pride, and my mother did everything in the house, with the help of a part time housekeeper: cooking, marketing, shopping, housecleaning, laundry – of course without the benefit of refrigerator, washer or dryer, dishwasher or other appliances that nowadays simplify these chores. She always kept a vegetable garden, she raised chickens and rabbits, and she found the time to sew our clothing, certainly for my sister, but also even for me.

**Cleaning Ladies**

We had a series of cleaning ladies over the years: I have retained only some of them in my memory: Madame Gallotini, who came to do the laundry: imposing, massive and good-natured. How small and shriveled she appeared to me when I chanced to meet her years later! My favorite part of the weekly laundry was the folding of bed sheets. My mother on one side, Madame Gallotini on the other; and me running from one to the other, being of no help, but exhilarated by the smell of the fresh laundry. I would slap at the sheets as they were stretched above me so that they would sink back down toward me, emitting even more of their heavenly perfume. This always took place in the basement, near the coal furnace, another marvel that I had attained the right to nourish with pellets of glistening anthracite.

And then there was Julie, whose memorable quote will always stay with me, "Women are no big deal, but men, they're nothing at all!", she would repeat it at the drop of a hat.

And that other one, whose name escapes me, whom the complications of housekeeping could plunge into the deepest perplexity. For example, while holding a dinner plate in one hand and a dish towel in the other, she needed to turn on a faucet. Oh, what gymnastics, raising the dish towel to eye level, turning the plate around, squinting at her forearms as they crossed first above, then below, until it finally dawned on her to put down whatever she had in one hand, turn on the faucet, and then pick it up again.

Then there were the little neighbor sisters. They did the bedrooms, and they would leave various presents on my bureau: drawings, cigarettes, books, seashells. At that time I was 16 or 17 years old; and although swelling with desire, I just didn't understand. Oh, the chasm that yawns between thought and action! They were so cute, all three of them!

## Pensions de Famille

Every summer before the war, to afford to take us out of town for the long summer vacations, my mother would organize a *"pension de famille"*, bringing along a half dozen little rascals around my age as paying guests. She not only had boundless energy, but also a very adventurous spirit. She always wanted a change of scenery: thus we went to Savoy, to the Vosges, to Brittany, to the Yonne valley, and one summer we even went to England. This arrangement made her work like a beast, but she did it again and again, every year. Our departures were always epic events. Not only did we have to take with us all our own provisions, but also everything for the boarders as well: which often included dishes, silverware, kitchen utensils, bed sheets and towels. On top of that, in those days, it was necessary to bring baskets full of food and drink, since the trip often took an entire day or night. And since we were going away for nearly three months, we had to bring along cats, rabbits and chickens. Ever since that time, I never travel with anything more than a small suitcase, except when I go to Georgia, where it's necessary to bring along everything, since there is nothing there to buy.

In general, my father did not accompany us. Every year before the Second World War he went "to take the waters" at Evian, and he would join us later. And in fact, he would seem to be in better health, with a rosy complexion, lively eyes and more alert. Now that I have reached his then age, I suspect that he had some rejuvenating feminine adventure with each trip to Evian, given that he was such a handsome figure right up until the end.

## Doctor Manoukhin

In those days many people went for an annual "cure", "to take the waters" as they said then, in numerous thermal spas in France and Europe. One went to relieve a variety of ills, and every spa had its specialty, People also went to undergo a preventative treatment to ward off tuberculosis, according to the beliefs of that time. That disease was the great killer of the pre-war years. It was everywhere, and it struck in all social circles. It was a rare family, no matter how sheltered, that did not count at least one victim. The fight against this plague affected everyone. We school children were mobilized every year to collect money through the sale of anti-tuberculosis stamps, and in our Georgian colony, the women organized collection drives, shows, dances and other benefit events the proceeds from which would go to defray the medical and sanatorium expenses of the sick among us.

My mother was very active in these efforts, which were often placed under her direction. She also got involved in individual cases, functioning as a sort of social worker, at a time when such a profession just barely existed. She gave of herself wholeheartedly: she kept in contact with doctors, organized hospital stays, chose sanatoriums, and occupied herself with financial questions. Through these activities she acquired a good amount of empirical knowledge regarding medical issues, and she ending up knowing a lot about various doctors. Among these she had a hero: Doctor Manoukhin.

He was a handsome man of about fifty, straight shouldered and bald, with a pince-nez on his clean-shaven face. Doctor Manoukhin had concocted an elaborate system in which mysterious rays that he concentrated on the spleen were supposed to accomplish miracles.

Imagine laboratory bottles and distilling devices full of mysterious, colorful substances, great orange glowing accumulators of occult forces, bluish tubes and tangled wires, all installed high up on a series of armoires and shelves, all linked to a sort of upside down funnel attached to the end of an articulated arm above a leather couch partially covered by a white sheet.

My mother believed wholeheartedly in those famous rays, not only as a treatment to stop the progress of tuberculosis and other diseases, but also as a fortifier. Thus every year she would drag us, my sister and me, to see Dr. Manoukhin for a "preventive" treatment, which consisted of a series of longer and longer sessions.

I see myself stretched out on the couch, my stomach exposed, my mother at my side, waiting for the Master to enter. He would appear, solemn, appropriately dressed in white, with a long wooden stick in his hand. With a ceremonial air, like a priest officiating before an altar, he would immediately face his bizarre apparatus, without even a glance at his patient. His face a mask of concentration, his pince-nez gleaming, he uses the edge of his baton to bend a metallic antenna sticking out from one of the tube fitted bottles in the direction of one of the copper accumulators enthroned high atop an armoire. With sharp crackling noises, long bluish sparks shoot out, bridging the gap between the antenna and the accumulator. The smell of ozone fills the room. We were all duly impressed. He would approach the couch where I lay stretched out, take my pulse, with his gold watch in his hand, and make me stick out my tongue, which he examined intently, taking notes in a thick notebook. Afterwards he would set the famous funnel just above my spleen, set a mechanical timer and announce the duration of the session – anywhere from three to ten minutes – and then leave the room with a majestic stride, his apparatuses filling the room with modulating buzzing and contrapuntal bluish sparks.

When the session was completed, he would return to free me and give us, my mother and me, entry into his inner sanctum. Dark walls, arm chairs and sofas in black leather, a massive mahogany desk covered with paperwork. Shiny instruments and mysterious volumes of books could be seen behind the glass doors of several cabinets, on top of which perched more bizarre apparatuses. He would take my pulse and check my tongue one more time, writing who knows what in his famous notebook. I was told to wait outside the door, and he and my mother would have a tête-à-tête for some minutes. Then we would go home, my mother once again reassured and encouraged, and her blind belief in Doctor Manoukhin and his astonishing system once again reconfirmed. This is something that I still have trouble understanding, since in all other matters my mother had a very sensible head on her shoulders.

Not only my mother, but also many other people were convinced of the beneficial character of those treatments, and not just laypeople, but members of the medical profession as well. The simple fact that Doctor Manoukhin was able to practice in Paris, even though he lacked a French diploma is proof enough of this. This was only possible because he had the sponsorship of a French doctor, under whose name the medical office was officially registered.

At that time in France, doctors in exile from Georgia and Russia, and I imagine all the immigrants in general, did not have the right to practice with just their foreign diplomas. They were required to pass the French examinations in order to have the necessary university degrees. And although they would have been able to pass the examinations that were concerned with medicine, with a bit of reviewing, there was one obstacle that stopped them all: *le baccalauréat*, first level university entrance exams of general knowledge. In truth, how many people, even though in possession of a baccalaureate, would be able to pass the exams again at the age of 45 or more? And anyway, one knows perfectly well that real education is essentially "what is left over once you've forgotten everything that you've learned."

In principle anyone, regardless of age, could present themselves for the baccalaureate exams, and take it under the same conditions as the 18 year old students. In practice this very rarely happened. Remember that before the Second World War one was old at 50, and at 40 one was already middle-aged! Even now, it is not customary for the French to take up higher education after the usual age, as one often sees Americans do, recycling themselves after having retired with 25 or 30 years of service.

Moreover, we now know that that type of exam cannot be considered in any way comprehensive and objective, first of all by the inevitable use of language, French in this case. Although many of the émigrés spoke French in a fluent way, their knowledge was superficial, so to speak, since they did not really have access to the extensive cultural baggage that all members of a group acquire automatically through family, school and society. And since one's world view is heavily influenced by one's language, apart from the formal content of knowledge on which the student was being examined, it was and it remains today very difficult for any student from a foreign country to totally grasp the underlying significance of all the words being used.

Thus, in general, our doctors in exile found it impossible to practice in France. But it was possible for them to do so under certain conditions in the overseas territories, where the lack of degreed professionals made for different regulations. As far as I know, the only one to take advantage of this situation was Doctor Tsintsadze, who was my godfather when at the age of 13, it entered my head, from I don't know where, to become baptized.

To my knowledge, Doctor Manoukhin was the only one to successfully circumvent these severe regulations. He had been able to convince at least one doctor of the value and the lack of risk in his treatment, so that this one would cover his practice and accept legal and medical responsibility for whatever actions were committed under his aegis. As for me, a child, I let myself be treated without really knowing why. Later on I was led to understand that these famous rays were supposed to stimulate the spleen so that it would produce more red blood corpuscles which were said to be qualitatively different from ordinary red corpuscles. These corpuscles, in turn, were supposed to be able to play a fortifying role in attacking harmful microbes, in particular those of tuberculosis, and even, in certain cases, - and here my mother would lower her voice mysteriously – cancer.

I don't know if those rays ever did me any good. In any case they did a world of good for my mother, at least psychologically; as for me, they didn't seem hurt me at all. Now that radiation treatment has become an integral part of therapy, perhaps Doctor Manoukhin was a viable precursor, in spite of all his charlatan trappings.

### My Wardrobe

We lived a strange mixture of poverty and wealth, of pride and conformity that was and still is the lot of certain émigrés. Poverty, or more exactly, the scarcity of funds, was something that I had no idea about as a child. After all, we never lacked for anything essential. My parents never desired more than what was necessary to live, and their spiritual life was just as intense as ever. Later on, after receiving my elementary diploma and entering high school, the economic situation began to weigh on me. Young people at that age are terribly conformist, in their attitudes as well as in their appearance. And my appearance was certainly distinct... not because I wanted it to be, far from it! But because since we were not able to buy many things, my mother sewed my clothes. And as she had a style all her own, they were definitely different! Often my schoolmates would make fun of me, and although hurt to the core, I developed a thick skin and pretended that these were exactly the clothes that I wanted.

I especially remember a pair of knickers that my mother had fashioned for me, a style which at that time was quite acceptable, even elegant, in certain social circles. But at the Lycée Michelet, not in the least! This type of pants is buttoned just below the knees, around which they puff out with enough extra room so as not to restrict movement, like a sort of sack. Naturally, my little classmates called them "pants to shit in". How conspicuous I was! I remember getting rid of them as quickly as possible! I was maybe 14 years old at the time, but the memory stayed with me for a long time.

During the war it got even worse, with the general scarcity of things. Who doesn't remember shoes with hinged wooden soles, as uncomfortable as they were ugly, which so many of us were forced to walk around in?

In the monotonous gray of those years, gray weather, gray, malnourished faces, gray clothing, one day the color red suddenly became the fashion. It began with some women's jackets of such a violent red that they could be seen approaching from afar in the generalized grayness.

What an eyeful! There were never very many of them, but they certainly made one take notice. They were so rich, so prosperous looking, those jackets! Among a whole mass of gray students on the "Boul' Mich'", we would stop, fascinated by the Color from the moment we would spy it at a distance, coming toward us. Hundreds of eyes would follow its path... those few young women wrapped up in their red evoked for us all that we didn't have, and we forgot for an instant our hollow bellies, our shoes with wooden soles, our patched up clothing, our gray city, the cold and the humidity that bore down to the bone, all these miseries and more!

At first it was only the classiest of young women that turned red like that, such as my buddy Marik du Troc, blonde and blue eyed, with a rosy complexion, always well dressed; she gave off with her entire person that little whiff of difference that immediately established her class. She was one of the first to appear in a short, well-tailored red jacket, a powerful, brilliant red. She certainly made a fashion statement from a long way off.

That was when I really understood why people in ancient times attached so much importance to the trade in purple, indigo and dyes, and why places that were able to produce these color products became rich and elegant. One irony of that world war: Roman history, the bane of all young scholars, came alive for me through color!

Quite soon the imitations began. You could clearly see that they were fakes, those bad copies flaunted by girls who wanted to be up to date without really having the means. That red wasn't really red anymore: it turned a bit orange, the dye seemed to be on the surface, the cut of the coat was clumsy, it was badly made, and the girls who hunched up in those imitations were themselves imitations with their dyed hair, their excessive make-up which could scarcely hide their faded gray complexion -- the general coloring of those years of hunger.

And under those fake coats one saw shabby skirts, blouses, shoes, all the accessories of people who had neither work, nor money, nor means to procure them, nor goals to work toward in that dead-end universe with a hopeless future.

I had a similar impression a few years later, upon my return from Spain: I had lived for more than two years in Franco's Spain, where there was still a great lack of food, old fashioned customs, drab, gray colors in the streets and inside the houses – except for the bull ring, of course.

Returning to Paris was like a visual revelation: when I had left, the city was still in the throes of the post war years, but during my short absence everything changed: and as proof, all the colors had come back! In the streets where innumerable neon signs dazzled one's view with their bad taste, in the homes where even the kitchen utensils took on an attractive allure of vibrant colors, on the inhabitants as well, especially the women, of course, who now had the means to dress in that inimitable French elegant fashion that still makes American women jealous 50 years later. It would take poor Spain quite a few more years to erase the image of the saying that "Africa begins at the Pyrénées", as was formerly said, and rejoin the colors and the relative prosperity of France and Europe.

And then one day, after years of limping around in shoes with wooden soles, or some other soles of unknown origin riddled with holes, years of feeling the cold in my feet that were permanently wet all winter from the rain that seeped in from top and bottom, of trying to make a difference by rubbing black ink onto those pathetic shoes in order to hide the worn out spots, after all of that, then, one fine day I somehow got my hands on a real pair of shoes, entirely made of leather, with real leather tops and thin soles, elegant and solid.

I was so dazzled by them that I immediately went up and shut myself into the attic of the house in Vanves in order to be alone with my treasures. There, under the skylight that was opened at night, I exalted in my unheard of luck, and scribbled in pencil these purple lines of doggerel. Fifty years later, I still preciously retain the original:

### Les Grolles

*Il les a pris, les a saisi*
*leur a collé du cirage blanc*
*Et pis j'te frotte et te refrotte*
*et que ça brille, c'est épatant*
*Elles le regardent en miroitant*
*te lui envoie un d'ces coups d'oeil...*
*" J'les ai cirées, j'les ai frottées*
*et ça reluit qu'j'en suis baba*
*Mes belles tatanes elles sont rouge sang*
*et elles rigolent de cirage blanc "*
*Un coup de lune par là-d'ssus*
*V'la mes doigts d'pied tout chavirés*
*Dans les étoiles, que j'vous dis*
*elles me port'raient si elles pouvaient*
*Et que ça brille, ça reluit!*
*J'peux plus toucher l'pavé*
*Pieds nus que j'me vais marcher*
*en les portant bien tendrement,*
*Des foyes qu'elles pourraient s'abimer*
*mes belles godasses que j'ai cirées.*

**The Shoes**

*He picked'em up, grasped'em tight— Slapped on white polish—*
*And then I rub, and rub again— And they shine so that's*
*wonderful— They look at him all a-mirroring— Flash at him Oh*
*such a look:— « I polished'em, I rubbed'em— And they shine so*
*much I'm all a-flutter—*

*My beautiful shoes, they are blood red— And they laugh thru*
*that white polish ! »*

*A Moon beam over all this — and my toes feel ready to faint—*
*In the stars, I'm telling you they would carry me if they but could —*
*And they shine, and they glitter— I wont have'em touch the*
*pavement— Bare foot I shall henceforth walk —Carrying'em ever so*
*tenderly— In case they could be damaged — My beautiful shoes I*
*have shined so bright!*

46

**Music and Nicolas**

We got our love for music from our mother. My father accepted music, and I suspect, with no offense intended, that he always remained deaf to it, as though it were one of those mysterious manifestations of the human spirit not everyone has the capacity to understand and appreciate. Music played an important role in our home. I mean live music, no matter how badly sounding from a mediocre piano played by clumsy fingers, or how badly warbled by uncertain voices. It was so much more intimate and touching within these limitations than those well-organized, high quality sounds that reach us so easily from all sides! It was the era of stammering radios, of 78 rpm discs made of fragile Bakelite, of mechanical phonographs, of cinemas that had just learned to talk. It was the time when the film, "Carnegie Hall", with Leopold Stokowski at the podium with its "living" sound transmitted via screen and loudspeakers, filled the crowds with enthusiasm, even those who normally had little appreciation for symphonic orchestras.

Perhaps we had a radio at that time, but I don't remember it at all, undoubtedly because it rarely broadcast concerts. But on the other hand, I clearly remember the day when a Georgian with the melodious name of Skonkoshiashvili, a party member, gave us an electric record player. What marvel of marvels! It was no longer necessary to crank up the motor, and the sound itself was so much superior! Our first records were the *Red Army Chorus* and *A Night on Bald Mountain* by Mussorgsky; we were amazed by the dynamic contrasts from pianissimo to fortissimo, contrasts that had been impossible on the old hand cranked phonographs.

But it was live music that remained our daily fare. Our parlor was dominated by a magnificent upright piano, large, heavy, ornamented, topped by candelabras, with a deep and powerful sound that bathed our neighborhood with its sonorous waves... so much the worse for them! – the corner

47

grocer would tell my sister, "Your brother plays so well! We can hear him all the way here!

Thus, my mother was the musician. I remember that I sang from an early age with my sister Nini, with my mother at the piano. Oh, nothing particularly complicated: The *Bells of Corneville* comes to mind, also, that Christmas carol that begins, *"Petit Noël, avec mysté-ére..."*

When my sister was six or seven, she began to take piano lessons, like all the girls from good families. As I was three years younger, and a boy, I was not included. But undoubtedly out of jealously as much as desire, I insisted on hitting the piano keys all by myself, so that by four or five years of age I also gained the right to take lessons!

As my sister got older, she gave up music to throw herself into the study of metallurgic engineering. She was part of the first graduating class of the Girls' Polytechnic School, which disappeared once women were fully admitted to the regular Polytechnic. But I continued and, at the same time as I was studying literature, I took classes in harmony, counterpoint, orchestration and composition, principally with Nicolas Stein, a flamboyant musician. I was his star pupil... which was not difficult, now that I think about it, since I was the only one who remained loyal to him throughout the years, given his very peculiar attitude toward the teaching of music.

The least that one can say is that our lessons were far from being regular or conventional. How many times did I arrive at his house at the prescribed hour to find no one there, or to hear a sleepy voice groan, "Excuse me, I overslept. Would you mind terribly much coming back next week? I worked really late last night!" It wasn't until later that I realized what it was that he called "work" was more often than not painting the town with some dancer. He loved women, to the great consternation of his wife, Sonia, who was also my piano teacher. As he had chosen to work with ballet companies, a world in which most of the men are homosexuals, the companionship of young women was something that he never lacked especially because he was very good looking, in the Russian style: broad shoulders, powerful chest, clean-shaven face, he also had the good fortune to wear his naturally silvery hair combed straight back, à la Leopold Stokowski. He was between 35 and 40 years old when I studied with him, and his appearance remained almost exactly the same right up to his elderly days.

Like any good Russian, he very much liked to drink, often to the point of not knowing anymore what he was doing or where he was, even and especially in circumstances where he had to make a good impression in his own best interests. A nihilistic character? Nerves? In any case, he had a definite genius for throwing away any opportunity to utilize his talents to their fullest. And that is perhaps why he always remained a satellite, so to speak, of the ballet maestros, either as an accompanist or especially as an arranger and orchestrator, tasks that he excelled in. And naturally, busying himself with the young ballerinas, a job that he was so fond of… and which often rewarded him in more ways than one.

In spite of all this, we managed to make contact once or twice per month, but then it wasn't a simple lesson, but a veritable marathon; often it lasted the entire day, from 10 in the morning until late in the evening. We went over everything: pianistic technique, interpretation, fingering skills, Buddhism, harmonic analysis, Gurdjieff, counterpoint, esoterism, science fiction, orchestration, art history, folklore… all of it intermixed with musical anecdotes, gossip about the celebrated dancers and ballerinas he worked with; mystical considerations which all led right back to his great love: Music with a capital M, center of the world, center of the universe, which throughout all his vicissitudes remained ever his great passion.

Thus Nicolas opened up unknown territory for me, he offered me unheard-of visions, he made me penetrate the great composers with all my senses… but I can't say that my musical studies with him were very solid technically. He was quite aware of this, and so to compensate, he had me take private lessons in harmony with a certain Professor Becker of the Conservatory, who was his absolute antithesis: dressed formally, precise, and seemingly without a trace of humor or imagination. I went to take my lessons with him at his ever neat and orderly apartment that perfectly reflected his total lack of personality: a real *petit bourgeois*.

That was during the war, in the wintertime. I would arrive at his house in the morning, let by his wife to the parlor where he gave my lessons, and where a coal stove occupied the place of honor. This was nothing unusual, since with the restrictions there wasn't any other way to obtain heat, even if the building had, in theory, central heating. Monsieur Becker would arrive, and without saying a word, would take a piece of kindling paper that was prepared in advance, bring it to the stove and light it with his cigarette lighter. Then he would insert the paper into the stove and without hesitation, without checking to see if the fire had caught on, he would turn to me and begin the lesson. In fact, the fire correctly caught on without fail: I had the feeling that the fire would never dare to back up into the room, with its ever so polished and precise décor! Soon discreet warmth began to spread, just enough to feel that the stove was functioning. Because it would never have been appropriate to get a roaring fire going: waste fuel? What a horror!

Without really being conscious of how cold I was, as the lesson advanced, I felt more and more uncomfortable. Thus, at the end of one hour, as soon as Monsieur Becker rose to signal the end of the lesson, I instantly ran out, and headed numb into the metro in order to warm myself up. In wartime Paris the underground tunnels of the metro were one of the rare places where the temperature was relatively comfortable: even the libraries and the cafés were glacial. In fact, it was not unusual for me to install myself on a bench in a station and stay there for an hour or two with a book, my lessons or a newspaper. I had my favorite stations, be it for the good lighting and the good condition or especially because they were perceptibly warmer than the others. La Concorde, on the Porte de Versailles–La Chapelle line, was one, also Saint Michel, which was often the meeting place for me and my friends, or Montparnasse...

Nicolas' home was, on the other hand, total chaos: sheet music parts open here and there, sheet music stacked up on the piano, books scattered all over, dishes and plates piled up in the sink or simply forgotten in some corner, with bottles filled to varying degrees and, naturally, overflowing ashtrays to the right and left.

His apartment was in Boulogne, on the seventh floor, with an open view of the Seine and the Renault factory. When I became an adult, or nearly, I would stop by from time to time, no longer as a student, but as a friend. As in the past, our discussions revolved around music, now washed down with wine and vodka. One wartime evening, as Nicolas and I abandoned ourselves to some rather strong musical libations, suddenly a magnificent bombing took place right before our eyes, right there outside our windows: the Allies were shelling the Renault factory in Billancourt!

I use the word "magnificent" advisedly, because if for a moment one reduced all the enormous human suffering and destruction to mere abstractions, the bombardments offered an astonishing spectacle of Sound and Light. (Is this where they got the idea?) Searchlights crisscrossing the sky, rumbling aircraft motors, flak tracing red, green, blue trails, flares descending slowly in groups, suspended by their parachutes –they were called Christmas trees, because of the resemblance in shape and brilliance, — the sparkling of the bursting shells against the black depth of the night, the deep coughing of the anti-aircraft

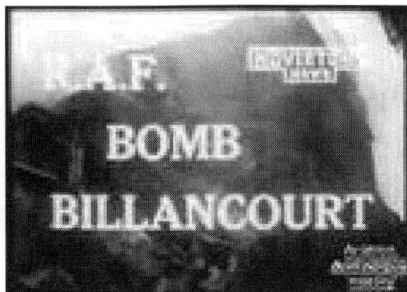

cannons, the crackling noise of a hail of shrapnel as it fell crackling onto roofs and sidewalks, the clacking of machine guns… and on top of that, that night from Nicolas' seventh floor windows, one could add the marvelous view of the fires that sprang up here and there, the glowing columns of smoke that rose, the scraps of iron and debris that flew up high even before the thunder of the explosions reached our ears through the general cacophony, Concrete music before it got its name, Wagnerian backdrops  for an apocalypse of the soul… and anyway, these were the allies, our friends, that were dropping bombs, thus they couldn't possibly harm us!

I believe that we went insane: yelling about the harmonies of the sounds that were reaching us, howling about the wonder of it all, Nicolas or I or both of us running to the piano to pound out booming chords in counterpoint to the explosive sounds so close, grinning at the emotions in us that came tumbling out with the blasts and explosions, singing to the tinkling splinters of glass shattering all around us,  we drank to the Allies, to the Music, to the airplanes, to the Absolute Spectacle that had been given to us to absorb…. And not for one second did we have the slightest feeling of danger.

The bombardment ended. The fires raged under our windows, the *pin-pon* of the fire trucks and the sirens of the ambulances lulled us, exhausted, drunk, we fell asleep. In the morning, we soberly took note that all the windows had been shattered, the furniture overturned, even the piano had traveled to the center of the room. The floor was covered with plaster and glass shards, the walls and the ceiling showed great gashes, and the façade of the building was pockmarked by shrapnel and machine-gun fire. We learned that all the inhabitants had taken refuge in the basement, and that only Nicolas and I had remained upstairs, spectator-participants, exposed like no one else, way up on our seventh floor.

Truly blessed are the fools, the drunkards and the musicians!

## The Ballet *Shota Roustaveli*

*Gontcharova's curtain for the ballet Shota Roustaveli*

It was my mother that conceived of the project to mount a ballet on the theme of The Knight *in the Panther's Skin*, epic poem from the 12th Century by the great Georgian poet Shota Rustaveli. And she succeeded in this enterprise, even if vested interests later forgot about the essential role that she played in the genesis of this grandiose project. It was a three-act ballet, nearly three hours in length, with a half dozen stars, about a hundred participants, a grand symphonic orchestra, sumptuous stage sets, dazzling costumes, amazing production values, the best contemporary composers and the greatest ballet master in Europe: Serge Lifar.

That was right in the middle of wartime. The center for ballet lovers in the Europe occupied by the Nazis was indisputably the Paris Opéra, where the *Maitre de Ballet* Lifar had managed to pull the ballet of the Opéra up from its traditional comfortable mediocrity in order to place it in the limelight. This was possible because of his talent, his social grace and his opportunism: at the time of France's defeat in June, 1940, Lifar was already at the Opéra; he remained there physically while nearly all the Parisians fled to the south.

It was into that nearly deserted Paris that Hitler marched triumphant – just once. He had wanted to visit the great monuments, of course, among them, the Opéra. Lifar was not present at that occasion, but he soon came to grips with the new reality, ingratiated himself with the powers that were, and soon became the uncontested maestro of the opera ballet, which he proceeded to transform into an incomparable jewel. [He was brutally fired at liberation for his "collaboration" with the Nazis, not to mention the jealousy that his position and success inevitably fostered during the war years, but was reinstated several years later.]

At the time the world of ballet was traditionally dominated by Russian émigrés. Thus it was natural that my mother went to that milieu in order to realize her dream. During the years she had never ceased to push her idea on every occasion and finally, around 1943, the project began to take shape, in great part thanks to a Georgian had made a fortune on the black market, and who wanted to be the principle patron, a certain Monsieur Beridze.

The official start was given during a large dinner in his sumptuous apartment at the Etoile, at the Arc de Triumph. I had been invited in capacity as a Georgian, a budding musician and assistant to Nicolas Stein – yes, he was there, in person – he had been working for a long time with Lifar as an accompanist, orchestrator, arranger, musical advisor and occasional composer. The host was Monsieur Beridze: in his sixties, portly, tortoiseshell eyeglasses, bald like most Georgians of his age, and not well dressed. H e stayed in the background and let the others talk, but one could clearly see that he was the patron, the most important personage of that gathering. There were a certain number of very important men and women in attendance, including Evgueni Gueguetchkori, our former Minister of Foreign Affairs, who had come in order to demonstrate the interest that the Georgian government in exile took for a work of such a national nature.

Serge Lifar was there, of course, good looking, athletic with a dark complexion – he made amazing leaps as the ghost in the ballet *Le Spectre de la Rose*!! It was he who made all the artistic decisions, who chose his collaborators, in short, who directed everything, besides being the choreographer: without him, nothing would have gotten done!

Nicolas Evreinoff was also there, the celebrated theorist of theater and author of plays that were performed all over the world. He was in charge of conceiving and writing the scenario of the ballet based on Shota Rustaveli's poem, in which he would interpose episodes from the life of the poet, as well as from the life of Queen Tamar, to whom Rustaveli had dedicated his opus. Also in attendance were Natalia Gontcharova and Larionof, Russian painters whose fame I was to understand only later. They were given responsibility for scenery and costume design.

Also there was the famous composer Arthur Honegger, as well as Alexander Tcherepnine, a Russian composer well known among Georgians: his father Nicolas had been the Director of the Conservatory of Tbilisi, where Alexander had grown up. Both of them liked to use Georgian folklore themes in their compositions.

My mother was there, and my master Nicolas Stein, as drunk as a skunk, staggering through the rooms, knocking over glasses and bottles, grabbing other guests to tell them all about who knows what in a slurring voice. Among other boorishness, he managed to topple a very valuable Chinese vase, shattering it in a thousand pieces. And yet he continued to drink by the glassful, in spite of my efforts to stop him, until he collapsed in a stupor. Through the persistent lobbying of Lifar he had been chosen as the third composer – given the length of the ballet, it had been decided to have one composer per act. However, by his conduct that evening, Nicolas had succeeded once again, in torpedoing his chances:

"Even if he were the greatest musical genius," exclaimed Beridze, "it won't do: I won't have him for anything in the world. We will have to find someone else!" Eventually the Hungarian composer Tibor Harsanyi was chosen to replace him. As for Nicolas, he went back to being what he had customarily been for Lifar: simple pianist-arranger.

It was at that dinner that the basic structure of the enterprise was established, that the financial questions were resolved, that the issues of responsibilities were finally decided, that the contracts with the principle participants were signed. And very soon the rehearsals began in a hall on the Champs Élysées.

The sessions took place daily from 10 in the morning until 4 in the afternoon. Lifar was always there, naturally. To assist him with the choreography, he hired an elderly Russian *maître de ballet* to function as a "memorizer", because of his prodigious memory that permitted him to store away in his head all of the details of movement, rhythms, expressions and not just the final product, but all of the intermediary stages as well. This was necessary because the art of dance notation existed in theory, but in practice it was extremely awkward and difficult to apply, and thus choreographers passed things down from generation to generation or from production to production solely through memorization.

Lifar had hired a Georgian dancer by the name of Petriashvili to demonstrate for him some typically Georgian dance steps, whenever he thought it appropriate to incorporate some in his choreography. He also had an entire troupe of dancers with whom he composed his choreography, among them Jeanine Charrat, who subsequently had a spectacular career as a dancer and especially as a choreographer, Olga Adabache, Vladimir Skouratof, Micha Resnikof, and many more whose names I no longer recall.

They were very versatile dancers that Lifar used as one uses stand-ins for the main actors in filmmaking: he created his choreography with them, but at the performances these roles were destined to be filled by ballet stars. As for music, at the piano he had Nicolas, with me as his assistant taking detailed notes and taking over his position on occasion.

Lifar's creative process was rather unique. Normally a choreographer chooses the music, or the music is composed especially for him, and it is on this music that he elaborates the dance steps. Here in the ballet *Shota Roustaveli*, the procedure went in reverse: Lifar created the choreography first, as the primary work, and the composers wrote the music using the schema established by the choreography. Let me explain:

For example, Lifar said to Nicolas: "This dance step will be lively and playful in a three-beat rhythm. Play me something." Nicolas then improvised a short melody.

Lifar: "No, that's too somber, lighten it up for me." Nicolas improvised something else.

Lifar: "That's almost it, try it a little slower." And so on, until Lifar felt satisfied.

Lifar: "Good, that's good, now give me a dozen measures in three quarter time," and it was by stringing together this improvised music and rhythms that Lifar created his choreography.

In this, my role was to take notation not of the musical notes, but rather the tempi, the rhythms, the number of measures per section. Sometimes I replaced Nicolas, and then it was I who improvised according to Lifar's instructions.

Once a choreographic number was finished and its musical structure established, this structure was sent to the composer, who wrote the music strictly observing the indicated rhythms and durations, as well as the expressive content of the choreography. I could never understand how they could ever compose anything good under those circumstances! Perhaps they just put down whatever came into their heads and for this reason they never bothered to later create orchestral suites based on this music, as was normally done.

The choreography and the production went forward at a brisk pace, completely ignoring world events, the war that raged worldwide, the bombardments in the outskirts of Paris, the poverty of rationing, shortages of transportation, electricity, of everything. And then, all of a sudden, the Allies' landing: June 6, 1944!

The rehearsals continued for a period of time, then they completely stopped. I thought that everything would be lost, that the ballet *Shota Roustaveli* would never be seen, since our backer, Beridze, had completely compromised himself with the Nazis. He escaped and the source of our money disappeared with him. Lifar was also considered a protégé of the Germans, so he would probably be arrested, or in any case, would lose his position. But he was never brought up on any charges, in part because the dancers and the personnel of the Opéra protected him, but also because it was well known that he was not at all political, that the only thing that interested him was his art! However, the *Comite d'Epuration* of the Opéra, charged with the task of purging the Opéra of collaborators, dismissed him of all his functions. He would return as ballet master at the Palais Garnier some ten years later.

In the autumn of 1945, more than a year after the halt of rehearsals, I received a phone call from Serge. "Yes, it's me, I have just managed to get some funding, and we are going to get back to work on *Shota Roustaveli*: do you want to join us as pianist and improviser?"

And as I was surprised that he hadn't called Nicolas, he said by way of explanation, "We had an argument." Nicolas, whom I felt duty bound to consult him before accepting Lifar's proposal, confirmed they had fallen apart.

The rehearsals resumed, but one could see that the money was rather scarce: the workplace was pretty shabby and the piano had a good quarter of its notes either missing or completely off-tune – which forced me into interesting contortions with my improvisations. From time to time the composers, to whom I was submitting my rhythm and tempo annotations, came to watch the creative process. Sometimes the rehearsals took place in Honegger's great studio on the Place Pigalle, sometimes at the home of one of the ballerinas, Ludmilla Tcherina, who would later become a movie star. Often Tcherepnine would come. There were also two or three more elaborate full dress rehearsals on the stage of a small theater.

After some six months of rehearsals, work was once again suspended, and my life followed other paths. One year later, to my surprise, I learned that the ballet had finally been realized, the scenes and the costumes created, the music composed, and the premiere taken place at the Opéra de Monte Carlo. That happened in the Spring of 1946, if I'm not mistaken, more than 3 years after its inception. The premiere was followed by three or four more performances, then the ballet *Shota Roustaveli* disappeared from the scene never to return.

Whatever happened to the music, the scenery, the costumes, no one seems to know. The choreography disappeared with the death of Serge Lifar, some 30 years later.

Now that Georgia is independent, it would be fantastic to find some Georgian or other well-to-do ballet lover like Beridze, who would accept to serve as patron, and revive the ballet *Shota Roustaveli* as closely to the way it was conceived in 1944. With some efforts it would be possible to recover Evreïnoff's libretto and stage directions, Gontcharova and Larionoff's costumes and scenery sketches, and perhaps the original music by Honegger, Tcherepnine and Harsanye. And if not, we don't lack for talented composers, such as Guia Kancheli, who could write new music.

As for the choreography, unless it was filmed at some point, it probably has been lost, since the ballet was never mounted again, and since the original dancers are undoubtedly no longer living or only have a vague and partial memory of it. But today there are many talented choreographers who would be delighted to create a new choreography on the theme of *Shota Roustaveli, Ballet en Trois Actes*.

Let's hope that someone will be found to take charge of such a project and bring it to completion, as my mother did more than a half century ago.

———————————

# 5. Encounters

It was in Paris in 1903 that my parents met – a neat, little sentence but full of significance. It took talent, effort, will power and inner vision for that event to take place. To begin with, look at a map. My father came from Lanshkuti, a small village in Georgia, at the foot of the Caucasus, way over there on the other side of the Black Sea. My mother also came from a small village, but far to the north, in the province of Orel, near Minsk in Byelorussia. In the former, a Mediterranean climate, oranges, palm trees, corn, mild winters, and in the latter, a continental climate, snow and ice six months of the year, potatoes, wheat....

But even more exceptional than the geographical convergence of these two creatures was their physical and mental development that made this meeting possible. In those times, it was not unusual for the Tsar's subjects to come to study or to make leisure trips to France, Germany and Italy. However, this was mainly rich nobles, or if not nobles, at least people from rich families, often members of the Koupetz class, a group of successful merchants who were often patrons of the arts and theater, for example, Diaghilev, the father of the Ballets Russes.

## On My Mother's Side

This was far from the case for my parents. Ivaneh Korenef, my mother's father, was a simple village parish priest. He was probably one of those Orthodox priests whose lives Gogol, Turgenev and many others have described for us, often in less than flattering terms. They were generally the sons of peasants who had shown an intellectual capacity that was a bit greater than that of their comrades, and thus were encouraged to continue their studies at the seminary. Their condition was somewhat higher in comparison to the peasants, with whom they nevertheless remained very close both in their lifestyles and customs.

In any case, the simple village priest that was my maternal grandfather had a magnificent baby grand in his simple *isba*, which one can imagine having been made of wood, with an earthen floor with a great tile-sided heating stove in the middle. He had his daughters take music lessons, and my mother Ina and my aunt Felichka were afforded an excellent education, including the study of French, just as for the nobility for whom this was almost a mother tongue, given the custom for them to learn French from the earliest age from governesses imported for this purpose from France. As a result, many of these nobles only spoke Russian with difficulty, just enough to be able to give orders to their servants.

That world is reflected in the works of the great Russian writers, who scattered their texts with French phrases and expressions. Reading these books in French translation, I found it annoying to see the text dotted with little numbers indicating footnotes at the bottom of the page. I knew quite well what these notes meant, for each time they were the exact same words. And yet, I couldn't stop myself from looking down at the notes, thus losing the rhythm of my reading, and I would hit the same sore spot once again: "In French in the Original text." Just thinking about it makes me see red even now!

In later years, having made progress in Russian, I wanted to buy *War and Peace* by Tolstoy in the original text. The bookseller handed me the volume, and I opened it to the first pages....

"You made a mistake, I told him as I handed the book back to him, I didn't want the French translation, but the original Russian."

"But that is the original that you're holding in your hands," he answered, smiling. And in fact, Tolstoy wrote the first twenty pages completely in French!

Of all the children of Father Korenev, my mother turned out to be the most musically gifted, and in fact, the most gifted in all subjects, while her two brothers proved to be good for nothing, as I came to learn. As a child I often heard her speak about her sister Felichka, who had been a mathematics professor in Tbilisi, but never about her brothers. I don't even know their names.

Ina not only learned French and music, but her father, the simple parish priest, allowed her to go study at the Sorbonne in Paris—this at a time when it was rare even for French women to dedicate themselves to such an activity. In fact, my mother was the first woman of any nationality to be enrolled in the Law School there.

How and by what means did Ina Ivanovna manage to get to Paris? I have very little direct information to retrace the exact steps through the political and social process that allowed her to gain that exceptional status. But I can conjecture. People don't really change over the years and my most vivid memories of her character, her capabilities and her attitude toward life in general and toward those around her, help me to imagine what her strategies were in those innocent times. In fact, it seems to me that she would have surely continued on her own course and accomplished quite a bit in her own right if it weren't for the strictures and customs of that time which erected nearly insurmountable obstacles for members of the fair sex. Instead, she found herself always in the shadow of my father, and was always occupied with her duties as mother of a family, though she continued with all her other activities.

All of this often occurred under very difficult circumstances, which nevertheless could be exciting, being out of the ordinary: Since my parents always stayed true to their revolutionary and patriotic activities, they were often forced to live abroad under extremely precarious financial conditions. But that was unimportant to them. Only the Cause mattered, for which all sacrifices were worthwhile.

As for the circumstances that permitted Ina to leave Russia, I can only speculate. In those days the Russian Empire was the only European country to require people wishing to leave to obtain permission to go abroad, what we would today call an exit visa. Once across the Tsarists border, on the other hand, anyone could go wherever he pleased: passports did not exist yet! My father often told me how, whenever he traveled in the world before the First World War, he carried with him letters and envelopes addressed to himself, to serve as identification papers. They were sufficient for crossing international borders!

With what money was my mother able to come to Paris to study? Travel was difficult in those days. There were trains, of course, but no cars, or nearly none, and naturally there were no airplanes, which in 1903 were still a dream. Thus the mass movement of people as we know it today, if only at vacation time, did not exist, since travel was so expensive. Unlike the nobles and the children of the Russian *kupetz* (merchant) class, my mother couldn't have had very much financial means, probably just enough to get to Paris and to establish herself. I am sure that the lack of money did not discourage her at all: after all, she is the same woman that, at the age of 85, hitchhiked across France because she didn't have enough money for the train and refused to ask her children for help!

As a student in Moscow, she had probably gotten herself involved in some revolutionary activities, which were the only means open to those who, seeing the misery of the Russian masses and the deep rooted iniquities of the Tsarist system, yearned to transform the society. Perhaps she was advised to leave the country for some time, and it was thus with the aide of her parents, friends and some revolutionary organizations, that she came to set herself up in rue Jean Goujon, in an apartment with five rooms, which she rented out in order to help pay the rent. Among the renters were Trotsky, a real gentleman, according to her, always polite and attentive, who paid all his bills promptly, and also Lenin, who finally left owing her two months' rent that he never paid.

What a pity that the Russian Communist Party has been officially dissolved! I would make a claim for those two months of rent which, with the accrued interest since 1903, would come to a considerable sum of money!

## On My Father's Side

My father's family belonged to the minor nobility, the *aznauris*, whose social standing was quite a bit higher than that of peasants, but whose economic situation at the end of the nineteenth century was probably not much better. Traditionally, there were only two categories of nobility in Georgia, the princes and the aznauris, which were also divided into two subgroups: the superiors, who were able to own serfs wherever these still existed, and those who did not have this right. Of course, as in all societies, there were still more variations, a subject I will not get into here. Our family, the Jordania, was the superior *aznauri* class, of relatively recent origin.

## Ancestors

If I know a bit more about my paternal ancestors, it's because my father, at the age of 65, wrote a small book, entitled *Livre à Lire en Famille*, or "Book to be Read in the Family". In it, he expounded his philosophy of life as well as the history of our family, which had been handed down to him orally from his father and by other older inhabitants of his village. His reasons for writing it, he said, was that each of us is in most part a product of our ancestors, but we nevertheless, as young people, aren't interested to ask questions about our forefathers, contenting ourselves generally with a few fairly superficial biographical facts. He decided to put down in writing for the benefit of us, his descendants, all that his own father had told him, which he had in turn learned from his own father, and so on from generation to generation, given that in our village of Lanshkuti, there were practically no written documents.

Around 1730, three brothers arrived by boat in Guria, a maritime province of Georgia. They came from Genoa, Italy, traveling on an Italian merchant ship. (Perhaps this is the origin of my passion for sailing and sailing ships? — given that no one in my past or present family has ever shown any interest in such an activity?) Their exact name has been lost, but I imagine that it was something like Giordano, the Italian form of our family name, and which is relatively common around the Mediterranean: Jourdain in French, Jordan in English, Jordaña in Spanish, etc. One of the brothers was a landscaper by profession, and the other two were merchants. They presented themselves at the court of Prince Gurieli, a real prince and head of the province of Guria.

One of the brothers left immediately for Mingrelia, the neighboring province. He set himself up in the village of Tsaicheli, where some of his descendants still live today. Another brother established himself in Arkhavi, where descendents of the Jordania family still live. As for the third one, he remained at the Prince's court, where he demonstrated his abilities as a warrior and as a companion, and where he fell in love with one of the court ladies. They were granted permission to marry, and on this occasion Prince Gurieli gave him some land and property in Lanshkhuti, as well as a certain number of serfs. All of the Jordanias of Guria are descendants of that individual, whose first name has been lost.

That first Jordania of Lanshkuti had four sons, probably born between 1750 and 1770. One of them, born around 1765, was called Katsoba, and he fathered just one son, who was named Redjeb, born around 1805. Redjeb was married around 1830, and he had three sons, Boudjou, Nicoloz and Yosep. Nicoloz, who was born around 1835, was my grandfather. He had two children, Noé, who was my father, born in 1868, and Goulnara, my aunt.

We don't know much of all the earlier generations of Jordania, as the oral histories don't afford much detail about them. In contrast, for the first Redjeb, my namesake, there are some very detailed traces.

## Redjeb

Only child of Katsoba Jordania, he was orphaned at an early age, and was sent to Mingrelia, where he was raised by his mother's brothers. As an adult, he returned to Lanshkhuti, where he was met with a strong hostility from the Jordanias of the village, probably because he came to claim his inheritance. Redjeb had a powerful, determined and direct personality. He did not let anyone contradict him or to stand in the way of his plans, including the other Jordanias, who feared him and ending up giving him some rather infertile land.

He cultivated the land and built a house on a raised platform (in Georgian, an *oda*). This *oda* still existed in 1914, according to a photo that I have before me.

*1914: the house with my Grandmother Cristiné, sister Atia, Father Noé, brother Andreika.*

Why on a platform? We don't know why. Possibly that area was marshy at that time, though it isn't anymore, or maybe because he wanted to be different from the others. In any case, it was the first house of that type in Lanshkuti itself, though there was already another Oda not far away, which belonged to a certain Matshutadze.

And there was even a certain rivalry that developed between the two men, and lead to dire consequences. This all happened undoubtedly during the period 1825-1830.

Since there were no birth certificates at that time, or marriage certificates nor other written documents upon which to establish a chronology, this is how my father managed to date family events: he could determine, he told us, that Nicoloz, my grandfather, was five years old in 1841. He was the second son of Redjeb, and he was thus born in 1836. His older brother Budju was four years older. As for his younger brother, Yosep, he died very young.

According to the usual run of things, Redjeb must have married no later than 1831. It was more than probable that he followed the customs of the time, and constructed his *oda* before moving in there with his wife, probably in 1830 and no earlier, since he would have been too young. Thus we arrive at the period 1825-1830 for his definitive settling in Lanshkuti.

He must have become an important personage, because with the advent of the Crimean War in 1853, he was given the responsibility of assembling a group of soldiers from his district, as was the custom. He distinguished himself enough to attain the rank of Captain.

On his return to Georgia, my grandfather participated on the side of the Russians, in the campaign against Shamil, the famous popular hero of the Northern Caucasus uprisings. Shamil fought the Russians for more than 40 years, until he was finally captured and sent to Saint Petersburg, where he died in golden captivity. The legend says that after having spent days and weeks traveling in horse-drawn carriages through the vastness of the Russian Steppes from the Caucasus all the way to the Baltic shores, he exclaimed upon being accorded an audience with the Tsar:

"Oh, you who possess such immensity why, oh why have your soldiers fought me for such a long time in order to capture my insignificant realm?"

It is interesting to note that right up until the present Shamil has been considered a hero by Georgians as well as by his own compatriots, even though the Georgians had fought against him alongside the Tsarist forces. Shamil and his followers were Sufis, a Muslim sect traditionally hostile to Christianity.

Redjeb was returning from an expedition against Shamil in the Caucasus Mountains, when at the edge of the forest he was hit by gunfire. He was killed instantly. Suspicion was not so much on Shamil's mountaineer fighters, as would be natural, but on Matshoukadze, the man who owned the other oda near Lanshkuti. The reason given being that Matshukadze had participated in the Crimean War and had gone on a campaign against Shamil, but everything that he did, Redjeb did better: He was more intelligent, more courageous, bolder. He had more successful exploits to his name and had attained a higher rank.

Overcome with jealousy, it is said, Matshukadze had hidden in that forest, knowing that Redjeb would have to pass by the edge of it, and had cowardly shot him down with a single bullet. As Redjeb died in military service, his widow received a government pension of 40 *moneti* per year. In that period a cow cost nine *moneti*, and a kilo of cheese 12 *moneti a*. To this day (1991 at this writing) and even though the nationally currency is still the ruble, no one uses that term, but rather the word "moneti", or coin.

An amusing note: when I was in Lanshkuti in 1991, one of the local Jordanias asked me quite seriously, "You know that it was a Matshukadze that murdered our ancestor. What would you do if you came face to face with one of his descendants?"

## My Paternal Grandparents

Here is how my father, without the aid of written documents, determined that his own father, Nicoloz, was just five years old in 1841: in that year there was a general uprising in Guria against the Russia occupiers — a documented fact. This was a spontaneous popular revolt, and in Lanshkuti the peasants wanted their immediate superiors in terms of social class, the Aznauris, to lead them, if only to serve as hostages.

Nicoloz told the story thus: "A veritable sea of people turned up at our house. But my father Redjeb wasn't there, and neither was my older brother Budju. So the people called for me, the next in line as representative of the family, since at that time women did not count in these matters. I was playing in the orchard with the other boys when my mother called me. She took me by the hand and led me to the demonstrators who immediately lifted me up onto their shoulders so that everyone could see that the Jordanias were with them.

When my father arrived he was furious. He chased the demonstrators from the house, and he punished me severely for daring to take part in that movement. I was barely five or six years old, but I remember the incident perfectly, and in detail." Whatever became of that protest movement, he never said.

My grandmother, Cristiné was fifteen years old when she married my grandfather Nicoloz, who was 27. Her father, named Chikovani, did not want her to marry, because he wanted to keep her at home to take care of him. Nicoloz and his parents, according to the custom of the time, put together many gifts, including a horse and carriage, and brought them to him. Mister Chikovani accepted them, allowed them to enter into his home, then chased everyone out and announced his refusal!

There was universal indignation, of course, since acceptance of the gifts in such a case, was tantamount to accepting the conditions of the bargain. But soon afterwards, and undoubtedly with the help of the object of Nicoloz's desire, as well as the complicity of certain members of the household, Cristiné managed to escape and thus the two were able to marry.

Just as his father Redjeb before him, Nicoloz very quickly became well respected in the village and the canton, and was often called upon to play the role of mediator, dispensing a sort of frontier justice, which was nevertheless accepted by all, including the authorities. He was always ready to be of service; he read a lot, but did not occupy himself with politics at all. However, he always kept alive the flame of nationalism and linguistic patriotism, which in Georgia were indistinguishable and which have always constituted the two faces of the resistance to foreign domination.

Cristiné, on the other hand, was illiterate, and remained so her whole life. My father wrote, however, that even though she could not read, she had an extensive knowledge of the language and of Georgian literary works, a great number of which she knew by heart, in particular, the medieval epic poem *The Man in the Leopard Skin* by Shota Rustaveli. And on top of that, according to my father, she had a style all her own, always precise, distinct, often poetic, and always perfectly appropriate to the subject at hand. He also wrote that anything good to be found in his style, he got from his mother.

Cristiné was, in some aspects, ahead of her time in her morale standards and her social attitudes. Here is an illustrative anecdote: A certain peasant owed a considerable amount of money to the Jordania family. Unable to pay, the peasant sent his ten-year-old daughter to Cristiné, to serve as an indentured servant. (Note that in Tsarist Rusia servitude was not abolished until 1861, thus old ways of thought were still extant).

Cristiné was indignant. She had the father of the girl brought to her and shamed him in front of everyone, saying that people are not animals, especially children, and one's own children at that. She said that no one had the right to dispose of them and to trade in them like so many vulgar possessions. She sent the little girl back home, after having showered her with gifts.

Cristiné demonstrated a humanitarian and democratic sentiment that, without a doubt, was not extremely widespread at that time. It was not only that the slavery of the serfs, just recently abolished was still alive in the mores, but also because the sale of boys and girls, be it by their own family or as a result of raids, had been common currency in all of the Caucasus for many centuries.

The boys were highly prized as future soldiers, especially in the famous Janissary Guards, who distinguished themselves brilliantly through the ages. As for the girls, they were highly sought after for their elegance and beauty in the Turkish and Arabic harems, be it as concubines or even as legitimate wives. In fact, in the 1950s, when I met young Egyptian people in Paris, where they had prudently taken refuge after the populist coup d'état that toppled King Farouk and his dynasty, I came to learn that many of them had one or more grandmothers or great aunts that were Circassian, Chechen, Ingush or Georgian.

**My Father's Education**

When my father was born in Lanshkuti in 1868, shortly after the elimination of servitude in the Tsarist Empire, noble titles and privileges still existed. These were not abolished until the fall of the Tsars and the proclamation of the Georgian Republic in 1918 by a decision of the assembly of Georgian nobility, which voluntarily gave up its traditional priviledges as well as most of its agricultural domain.

But at the end of the 19th Century there was little economic or social distinction in our village. Whether one was a peasant or an Aznauri, at that time it was nearly impossible for a young Georgian to gain access to higher education. To begin with, the Georgian language was forbidden in the existing schools. The obligatory language of instruction was Russian. This already presupposed that a student would be of a relatively high social class, since simple peasants and workers only spoke Georgian, and often only the dialect of their own province, not the so-called "classical" Georgian of writers, poets and men of letters.

Thus, my father wrote that from the age of twelve he did not live with his parents except during the school holidays, because the closest high school was at Ozurgueti, the main town in Guria, about 75 kilometers away. He went there on horseback, undoubtedly loaded down with sacks of provisions and food, without which his mother Cristiné would have never let him leave. In fact, when my father became President of the Republic of Georgia, some 40 years later in 1918, that august title did not stop Cristiné from coming often to Tbilisi, an entire day of train travel, loaded with all sorts of foodstuff, worried as always, that her son the President would not have enough to eat!

Previously my father had received rudimentary instruction at the parochial school, where he had learned to read, write, and do math, plus a religious-superstitious mumbo-jumbo that attempted to explain physical phenomena in magical terms. I remember clearly how he told me of his marveling joy at his discovery years later that thunder and lightning were not the manifestation of divinity, but rather natural phenomena that were part of a scientific explanation of the world.

One can imagine the avidity with which that boy, with his open and curious spirit would learn about the things that remained unknown to those around him in his social milieu. It was his eagerness to learn that brought him inevitably to the seminary in Tbilisi, the only means open to young Georgians to pursue higher education. Stalin would follow the same path some fifteen years later.

But let us read my father's own words in order to better appreciate the flavor of these remote times.

*******************

# A Child's Changing View of the World
# in 19th Century Tsarist Georgia

*Excerpts from Noé Jordania's book of memoirs*

I was born in Lanshkhuti, district of Ozurgueti, province of Kutaisi, Georgia, on January 2, 1868. I didn't know the Russian language when I entered Lanshkhuti's elementary school; I only knew Georgian. And in the first grade in that school, as well as in the school in Ozurgeti, which I attended from 1877 to 1884, I had only two primers: in Georgian, Deda Ena(The Mother Tongue), and in Russian, Radnoi Slova (Native Words). I heard that there existed another kind of primer in the Georgian language, The Doors of Nature, but I couldn't find it anywhere and had no idea of its contents.

I remember that one day in 1879, when I was 11 years old, I was walking near the barracks of the Georgian militia in Lanshkhuti, when I heard someone calling my name: it was Kondratin Jordania, a militia man who was a relative of mine. "Come over here, he said, I'll give you *The Doors of Nature.*" I rejoiced, ran over, and saw that he had in front of him a basket full of boiled beef. He took a big piece, gave it to me, and said: "Here you are, that's better for you than *The Doors of Natur".* I was awfully disappointed, threw down the meat, and ran away.

Another year went by. I carefully studied the Russian primer, as I was afraid the same thing might happen to me that happened to my friend Khilashvili, who was thrown out of school because he couldn't learn by heart in Russian the poem "Ptshelkina Rasvekax" (*The Questing Bee*). This method of learning was very hard for us, since the Georgian population didn't know Russian, and we the children had to learn Russian poems totally by rote, without even understanding the words. This is why our homework was such a torture.

One day our Russian teacher got sick, and a substitute Georgian teacher replaced him. "To keep you busy," he announced, "I'll read to you from a Georgian book." This book turned out to be *The Doors of Nature.* We heard in Georgian descriptions of various areas of Georgia and Georgian verses! When he finished and was about to leave, I ran up to him and asked him to lend me the book for a few days. He acceded to my plea and, overjoyed, I ran home.

I immediately started reading. The book astonished me. I was particularly fascinated by the explanations of natural phenomena: rain, wind, thunder.... I couldn't believe what I was reading. I would read each passage several times. I had been convinced, like everybody around me, that these phenomena were caused directly by God: When He wants rain, it rains; when He wishes for good weather, there is good weather. And now, all of a sudden, God has nothing to do with all this! God disappears; He is replaced by the forces of Nature!

I had been convinced that thunder was the noise of St George's horse galloping in the sky; and it turns out that it is not St George, that his horse has no relationship with the phenomenon of thunder! There and then I asked myself the question: Does God exist, and where is He? From that day on I never felt the same; I felt ill at ease, and these kinds of thoughts tormented me.

One day, because of rain, we remained in the classroom during the recreation period. I stood up and addressed my schoolmates: "Listen to me. I'll tell you something new".

The children stopped fooling around, surrounded me, and begged: "Tell us! Tell us!"

I blurted out: "You know something? There is no God!"

What an outcry from all sides: "What are you saying! How dare you! God will punish you! Ask forgiveness right now!"

I became ashamed. I became afraid of God, but I hid my feelings while nevertheless saying to myself: "Forgive me, oh God. Don't punish me for what I said." And I hit myself on the cheeks with my fist several times in penance.

But the unrest in my soul didn't stop with that incident. Disquieting thoughts bothered me, and I continued being interested in natural phenomena. I really wanted to know if God existed. I questioned myself on this subject, yet at the same time I was attending all church services and confessed twice a year—in short I behaved like a true son of the church. But my thoughts disturbed me and knocked on my soul, pushing me to search for answers. From that time on I saw that I was tearing myself away from the commonly accepted beliefs and, like a baby bird fallen from the nest, remained alone, crawling without road or direction. I couldn't go back to the old, nor go on to the new. I wasn't sure what to do. I saw that everybody around me lived and thought alike, that they didn't distinguish themselves from each other by their way of life, morals, or worldview. Now, among them I felt like a stranger. I would have loved to be like them, but despite my sporadic efforts I couldn't do it: I couldn't run from myself; I couldn't free myself from my questioning. The school on Ozurgeti didn't satisfy me, and in my few books I couldn't find answers to my questions. Thus when I finished my elementary education, I announced to my parents that I wanted to continue with my studies in Tbilisi, the capital of Georgia.

My mother got angry: "What? He is my only child, and I should loose him?" My father remained silent, but it was clear to me that he was not against my desire, if only he could manage to cover my expenses at the seminary and the boarding house. I asked our village priest, Baramidze, who knew how to talk to people, to speak to my mother. "Your son will become a priest, he will pray for you and save your soul. What can be better than that?" he told her. And with this he broke her negative attitude. To my father he said, on the contrary: "Your son becoming a priest? Don't you be afraid; that will never come to pass!"

My father succeeded in selling a piece of property for 80 rubles, and we traveled to Tbilisi. I entered the seminary and settled in a boarding house for 10 rubles a month. That was in 1884. I was 16 years old.

One day, when I was strolling in the streets of Tbilisi in order to get to know the town, I chanced upon old books that were being sold in the street. I ran to the stack, and suddenly noticed a large book with the title *God in Nature*. I don't remember the author's name. I treasured it for many years, and left it in my library in Lanshkhuti when I was forced into exile by the communists long afterwards. I read it several times with the help of Chubinashvili's dictionary and came to be convinced that God was synonymous with Nature itself: separate from Nature, as a being with a white beard sitting on a throne, he didn't exist. This thought calmed me, and in that state of mind I spent the first year in the seminary.

In my second year, again disturbing thoughts invaded me. If the master of nature is nature itself, then who must be master of the people? It was commonly thought in those days that the master of the people was the Tsar, and that the Tsar was anointed by God himself. But if there is no God, then who, with what authority, put the Tsar on his throne? I couldn't understand it. I felt that once again I was "falling from the nest". I tried not to think and to free myself from such disturbing notions.

I read everything that came into my hands. It was then that I met Zakharia Chichinadze, who had masses of books in his home. He promised to lend me some. He asked what I was interested in, but I couldn't explain my doubts. I didn't want to reveal my ideas, but at the same time I couldn't hide them either. I told him in general what interested me, what bothered me. He gave me two back issues of a Russian magazine, cautioning me not to open them in public and asking for their return as soon as I finished reading them. I couldn't wait: despite his advice, I opened them on my way home, in the street, and read the name Karakol. The articles in the magazines were a revelation to me: I was not alone with my upsetting thoughts! The magazines clarified my notions: the Tsar had the same kind of imaginary authority as God. I put them on the same level. Atheism and Republicanism in my view became neighbors.

I always had the character trait that as soon as I learned something new, I had to share it with others. I particularly liked to talk about this in our village. I remember a particular occasion when I came back to Lanshkhuti after having read *The Doors of Nature*. I went straight to the small hill in the field in front of our house, known as "the hummock of thought", where the Jordanias were wont to meet to talk, gossip, discuss, joined by whoever happened by. I went up to the top of the hummock, and little by little neighbors and passers-by gathered around me. I started explaining the meaning of nature and its workings. The young people were not interested, and soon scattered, but the elders listened with great attention.

When I had finished, one of them exclaimed: "Glory be to God! How did he arrange all this so well! If He had to take care of all the details by himself, what kind of God would He be?" And the man went on and on in this vein.

Now, when I remember this incident, I think it was a genial solution of the problem: it was the conciliation of God and Nature. But at the time, it impressed me, but not enough to make me change my opinions. Later I learned about the struggle against the Tsar and his oppressive government, and I wanted to bring this question to the Hummock of Thought. But it was much harder to speak about this question than to explain about rain and thunder.

One day I read in the newspaper Iberia an article about Thomas Edison's invention, the electric lamp, with which it was possible to light up a whole garden. As soon as I came back to Lanshkhuti, I told about this invention on our hummock. Everybody was astonished. Finally an elder exclaimed: "Blessed be God! What won't our Russian Tsar think of!" I was flabbergasted. I hadn't said a word about Russia or the Tsar, I had talked only about America and Edison. Later I understood that for the common people, everything good happens only thanks to the Russian Tsar.

This belief in the Tsar's goodness was reinforced at that time by the following event: in the years 1886-1890 the governmental Director of Forestry was a certain Kikadze. He declared that all private titles to the forests were invalid and required their transfer to government ownership. Several lawsuits began. In this quarrel the peasants sided with the government because Kikadze's agents cleverly spread the rumor that if the government won these suits the forests would be turned over to the peasants. Naturally our Gurian peasants made an alliance with the government against our Gurian landowners. Thus began an intense propaganda in favor of the Russian Tsar. In front of such a perceived self-interest of the people no-one could say anything against the Tsar and the government.

Because of that our new ideas were accepted only by the intelligentsia and the well-to-do youth. I couldn't come out against the Tsar and the Russian government on our hummock, since all the Jordanias were landowners and quarreled with the peasants on that subject. If I did, the peasants would have taken my words as a defense of the Jordania's interests.

It is through Russian literature and pamphlets that I got acquainted with revolutionary ideas. At the same time it is the Georgian writings that awoke in me nationalistic ideas and patriotic yearnings. However only in Akaki Tsereteli's poems could one feel that Georgia should be free, should become an independent nation. All the other demands dealt with questions of everyday life such as Georgian schools, Georgian literature, limited regional autonomy etc. In those times in Georgia nationalist movements had no reality.

Everyone dreamed of learning Russian and, having finished school, to find well-paid employment. The Georgian language was considered only good enough for the family and friends. No one could make a living knowing only this language, which counted for nothing in the Russian-dominated administration. In addition, for many people, and particularly the Gurians, the fact that Georgia was on the border with Turkey and always menaced with invasion led them to be happy to have Russian forces stationed on that dangerous boundary.

The only malcontent was the Prince Gurieli, titular head of the province of Guria, whose administration had been displaced by a Russian one. My friends in Ozurgheti, who knew personally the Prince Gurieli, told me that he was dreaming of the return of the old order, particularly in the border towns of Akhaltsikhe and Akhalkalaki. The Prince's dream went totally against the wishes of the people. The Gurians were still suffering from the awful custom of Gurieli's henchmen rounding up by force young men and girls and taking them to Turkey across the Tsholoti river to sell them. The girls in particular were much appreciated by the Turks, and they fetched a high price!

In Ozurgeti I lived in a family which was involved in the selling of those captives. Since the head of the family was a relative of mine, I was not afraid of finding myself in their company. This was in 1876, and until the Russo-Turkish war a few years later, there were still cases of selling young people across the Tsholoti river. Before I went to Ozurgeti I was terrified that somehow I would be caught and sold to the Turks. This fright diminished after the Russo-Turkish war began, when Ozurgeti was full of Russian soldiers and military operations began on the border.

I recall an event which confirmed the participation in this business of the militiaman Kondratin Jordania. After the battle of the Tsholoki river, the Russian army advanced in Adjaria-Kobuleti. A part of the Gurian contingent, under the command of Anton Kartsivadze, was quartered in Artvin. Anton and his platoon received a dinner invitation from a local family. The guests were greeted by a young woman who had prepared for them a Georgian dinner. When there were all seated at the dinner table, Anton looked closely at the young woman, blanched, and fell unconscious. His buddies picked him up and put him in another room, thinking he had passed out from too much drinking. But the young woman understood immediately what happened, went to him, and attempted to calm him:" I have long ago forgotten the past. You can see that God did not treat me badly. I am so glad to again see you Gurians!"

It turned out that this young woman, daughter of a Gurian peasant, had been captured and sold as a slave by this very Anton Kartsivadze, acting on behalf of Prince Gurieli!

When Kondratin Jordania, who was a member of the platoon and had been a witness, described the scene, tears would come to his eyes and he would exclaim: "What a marvelous soul Georgian women have!"

Growing up in such an atmosphere, the Gurians could not even conceive of a free Georgia. For them Georgia consisted solely of Khartlie, one of the provinces, and perhaps sometimes with the addition of Kakhetia, another province. Their main preoccupation was how to defend themselves against the Turks. The Gurians did not entertain good relations with the Russian civilians and the Russian administration, perhaps in part because of the language barrier. Speaking only Georgian, they could not communicate directly, and had no confidence in them. But they respected the Russian military, officers and men, and even pitied the simple soldiers, who in those times were treated abominably by their superior officers. Oftentimes I have seen some Gurians standing near their vegetable patch calling "Ruski! Ruski!" to give them fruits, vegetables, or other victuals. The Russian soldiers also behaved very nicely to the people, and I never heard of mistrust or animosity between them. But there were often clashes between Gurians and the Russian police.

I clearly remember the following incident: a new Russian representative had been named to Lanshkhuti. One day that character got into insulting and swearing at some peasants from his balcony. A crowd assembled, seized that individual, and beat him half to death. A big scandal ensued. Soon trooped in the district representative, the governor of the province, and other dignitaries. Telegrams announcing that the Revolution had started in Lanshkhuti were sent hither and yon … But things calmed down. The local representative was re-assigned elsewhere, and the powers that be issued a directive to all bureaucrats forbidding them to insult any Georgian. Those who had beaten up the Russian representative were not punished in any way.

In general, I must say that in Guria the people didn't like the Russians and their administration, but liked the presence of the Russian army, which they held in high esteem. Given these feelings, it was impossible to approach the people with new ideas on the social, political, and national levels. This depressed me. In summer, when I was compelled to live in our village, I felt estranged, as if I were a guest.

In Tbilisi, on the contrary, in the atmosphere of my study circle, I had the possibility to learn more and spread my ideas. At first I was just a member of such illegal circles, but later it was I who organized and lead some of them. Our subject of study were the social and political questions. I buried myself in books. Seminary studies gave me no satisfaction whatsoever. I loved history, and our textbook, by a certain Chernikovsky, gave no idea of the history of Russia or Europe. In the seminary we studied Russian literature only up to Pushkin, and of what came after him no one knew anything. Of Georgian literature, not a word, with the exception of some writings by the Georgian pope Gavriel, which our teacher Tedo Jordania read and explained in class; but even that little was in Russian.

We were allowed to check out from the library textbooks only, all the others were forbidden. If caught reading forbidden books from whatever origin, the seminarians were severely punished, and of course I spent my time reading forbidden books- In choosing my readings, I absolutely discarded *belle-lettrisme*. I didn't like books of fantasy or imagination; I read only books of learning. The only novel I read was "what to do?" by Chernishevskov, and this only because he was an authority in revolutionary circles, and because in his book are described the lives of noted revolutionaries. This one-sidedness of my studies can be explained by yet another circumstance: it was a reaction against the fantastico-superstitious atmosphere in which I spent my childhood.

This is worth a closer look: all the villagers in Lanshkhuti, and probably all the Gurians, had a fantasmatic view of the world. They were convinced that the universe was populated by invisible beings that were constantly fighting against the humans and confusing them as for their destiny. Who were these beings? They were demons, devils, monsters, ghouls, incubus, succubus, witches, warlocks and many others. The children were tormented by devils, and the adults by devils and all kind of other entities.

I always thought about devils and was afraid of them. I was never at peace. One evening one of my friends disappeared for some time. When he reappeared in the morning, I asked him what happened: "My mother sent me to the mill," he recounted- "It was dark. After I got inside, I heard noises and cries. "Who's that?' yelled someone, and grabbed me. Suddenly, from all sides devils jumped out, who started beating me. I managed to reach a corner, took out my knife, and tried to fend them off. No words came to my lips, so that I couldn't pray, even though mama told me that I shouldn't forget to recite my prayers since there were always devils at the mill. Some time went by, I don't know how much. Mama became worried, and came to get me with a candle. As soon as the devils saw the light they disappeared. Then prayers brought me to my senses and put me on my feet."

As soon as I heard this tale I stopped playing, ran to my mother, and begged her not to send me to the mill. She reassured me: "But of course not, child, how can I send you alone to the mill? Even in daytime I won't let you go. These despicable devils love the mill and hide in the gears and wheels, but they are afraid of light."

Another incident: one day four of us youngsters were returning home from Ozurgeti. We had only one horse, which we rode two by two in turn. We had reached the Netavi river when the sun went down. To shorten our way I and another boy went through the fields, and the other two continued on horseback along the road. We reached the river, but as soon as we stepped on the bridge we heard a voice: "Don't cross!" and someone or something jumped in the water. "The devils found us!" we cried, and frightened we ran back. We met our friends, told them what had happened, and we decided to return to Ozurgeti rather than risk crossing the river. We were on our way back, on foot and frightened, when we met a peasant with a hoe on his shoulder. "Where are you going," he asked. "Weren't you going to the river?" we told him everything, and he answered: "You're right, these despicable devils like to lurk around the bridge. But come with me, I'll help you cross the bridge. With this hoe I'll break some devils' heads if they dare attack us."

So we walked behind him, with our hearts beating hard from fright. We reached the bridge. We were scared to go further. The peasant got so angry with us when we hung back that he almost hit us with his shovel. He made us cross. As soon we were over the bridge we broke into a run and didn't stop until we reached Lanshkhuti.

When, still trembling, I told my mother of this adventure, she brought me for two weeks running to an old crone who, with prayers and incantations, cured me of my fear.

In Lanshkhuti the rumor spread that a certain old woman used to ride around astride a jackal. That was an unmistakable sign that she was a witch. A town meeting was convened, and some thirty men and women affirmed that with their own eyes they saw her sitting on a jackal! At the end of that meeting the old woman was chased away from the village. We never saw her again.

Ten years went by. I was back from Tbilisi when a certain Yofan Bolkvadze, who had been the principal accuser of the old woman, came by to visit my father. After a while he asked Yofan: "This is now an old story, but tell me: was it true that the old woman could sit on a jackal?" Yotan smiled, and answered: "Niko, you are a wise man. How can you ask me such an asinine question? Where did you ever hear that a person could sit on a jackal? That woman was my neighbor. I was tired of her. She was always abusing me, throwing garbage in my garden, bugging me in every way possible. I resolved somehow to get rid of her.

One morning I got up very early. There was a layer of fog hugging the ground. I saw the old woman going along the road, or rather the top half of her, the bottom half practically hidden by the mist. I don't know why I thought of it, but I yelled: "Why are you sitting on a jackal, caracoling on the road?" She got frightened, tried to run away from me, but I kept repeating that she was sitting on a jackal. Hearing the commotion the neighbors came out, and from a distance it did look as if the old woman was sitting on a jackal! The rest you know." Hearing that story, I laughed heartily (just at that time I had been reading about the phenomenon of mass hallucination), but ten years before I firmly believed with the peasants in the absolute truth of the event.

There were many other stories of that kind, and I believed all of them. Such was the kind of atmosphere in which I spent my childhood. What was real made no impression on me, but everything fantastic worried me in the extreme, influenced me strongly, and I took these fantasies for reality.

In those times by chance I read a book called *Karamaniani*. Reading it, I was flabbergasted: how many fantastic things happened in the world, that I knew nothing of! I looked for similar books of fantasy, I

*Encounters*

believed everything in them and read them with great pleasure. It is only after I read The Doors of Nature, which turned around my religious beliefs as well as my trust in those other books, that I wondered about myself and about how stupid I had been to believe in those tales.

It was in that state of mind that I arrived in Tbilisi and started collecting strictly realistic writings. I immersed myself in scientific, sociological and historical texts. After a couple of years I chose for my field of study the social questions, leaving aside science. But I was stewing in my own juices, since I had no possibility of discussing my ideas with anyone. There was only one place where I had a public that could listen to me: the Hillock of Thought in Lanshkhuti. But even there I met with great difficulties, since it was impossible to approach the people with many of my new ideas....

*Later my father left the seminary and registered in a veterinary school in Warsaw... but even though he always liked animals, I well know this was but a ploy to get to Poland, which was then part of the Tsarist Empire, to continue his revolutionary and nationalistic activities, a path he had followed from an early age.*

Noé in 1897

83

## My Mother's Education

As for my mother, I don't know exactly what schools she went to, but one must think that she too showed an exceptional capacity, since she not only succeeded in graduating from the Gymnasium, but also was able to go to Paris to further studies at the Law School. In 1900 the fashion was of wide flowered hats —true gardens!—, long skirts down to the ankle, bodices severely buttoned. The story goes that when my mother, thus adorned, would arrive at the Sorbonne amphitheater, the other students, all male, would stand up and lead her to the place of honor: a woman, and more so a pretty woman, at law school!

## Love and Politics

It is then that my father arrived in Europe as a delegate of the Georgian Social-Democrats to the 1903 International Socialist Congress. He first went to Switzerland, where the Congress was to take place. But the Swiss, afraid of those "rabble-rousers", refused permission, and finally it is in London that the Congress convened.

At that occasion Lenin, who always preached the principle of authority coming from the top, offered my father to join his faction: "You Georgians don't really know our Russian people," he said. "The only way to make them progress is to use the *knout* (cat-o'nine-tails). They have no sense of their own interest, no willpower, no spirit of initiative or organization. Left to themselves they'd only talk for days on, complain, get drunk. They need a hard, severe, demanding master who'd know how to dominate them in order to make them progress."

It is this doctrine, as we well know, which applied wherever the communist party was in existence… until its demise in the East in the 1990's. But this of course went totally against my father's democratic principles. He answered: "For us, Georgian socialists, it is to the contrary all the members of the party who decide by majority vote doctrines, principles, actions, and choose leaders and delegates. I'll talk to my fellow delegates, since we never do anything without consultation, and I'll give you our answer in a week." The answer was of course negative.

Soon after this incident, at that Congress took place the historical schism between extremists and moderates, communists and democrats, Bolsheviks and Mensheviks, between Lenin, Trotski, Stalin on one side, and on the other Plekhanov, Mdivani, Jordania, Kerenski.

My mother also was at the Congress, but she didn't meet my father at that occasion. Since he was going to Paris, the legend says that either Lenin or Trotsky advised him to take a room in the apartment of Ina Ivanovna, a young Russian woman who rented to Russian revolutionaries to help pay the rent. And this is how my mother and father met, appreciated each other, loved each other, Noé quickly seduced by Ina's long hair which reached below her waist, and which she wore thus until she died at age 90. My mother was then some 27 years old, and my father 38.

---

# 6. The Chateau in Leuville

Memory is often irrational. An event, a period of life can come back to you stripped of the emotional attachments that surrounded it, permeated it and gave it life, and it simply appears as a naked image, inexplicable, absurd in its isolation, like the French poet Charles Cros' salted herring stuck by a nail to the naked wall. And then there are the false memories that one knows perfectly well to be inexact, but which can push out the so-called "real" scenarios. So-called because perhaps the real "real" consists finally in whatever refuses to disappear?

In my case, it still seems to me to this day, that I spent all of my school holidays in Leuville, even though I know full well that it is not true. During the summer vacation, July, August, September, my mother always took us far away, with the young paying guests that she brought along to help with expenses. For the Christmas holiday, it was too cold to stay in the big, icy rooms of that unheated chateau. That leaves only Sundays, the Easter holiday and other springtime holidays.

**The Little Train**

When I was a child, perhaps until around 1936, one traveled to Leuville by means of a small train that began at the

Porte d'Orléans. It was an authentic little narrow-gauge train, pulled by an authentic miniature steam locomotive that ran alongside the national highway, through villages and small towns along the sidewalk, cutting through streets and

pathways without the benefit of protected grade-crossings. From Linas, some five kilometers before Leuville, the train went across the open land to meet up with the Orge River, which it followed until the terminal at Arpajon, a small town famous for its covered market with its immense roof of rough intertwined roof beams dating from the Middle Ages.

The train moved so slowly that it took nearly three hours to cover the 17 kilometers from Porte d'Orléans to the small station at Leuville. One could jump off the front of the train, have a drink at a café along the tracks and get back on the back of the train, without even rushing. Once at the Leuville Station it was possible to take a path through the fields and climb the gentle slope toward the lower walls of the chateau, through the apple orchard that belonged to it. Stepping through a postern that always stood open, we would pass through the vegetable garden and climb up the stairs through the supporting wall of the chateau's inner yard. It was a pleasant, bucolic walk of at most ten minutes.

Just before the war, the small train was discontinued in an effort at modernization and replaced by busses, most of which stopped along the national highway, high on the other side of the village. Some stopped in the square in Leuville at the entrance to the chateau, which was very practical for our older people. With the coming of war, the busses disappeared, and since the little train had so enthusiastically been done away with, the only means of public transport left was the Brétigny train, seven kilometers away on foot.

## The Village

At that time Leuville was a small farming village. Along the long main street were, on one side, small merchants and small truck farms that were sandwiched in, with their narrow plots of land extending in back all the way to the national highway some 500 meters away. These were small truck farms. Some of the farmers also had land on the other side of the hamlet, but none of these fields were very large, and they were mostly plowed by horsepower, though there were a few tractors about.

On the other side of the street, where the land sloped down, there were many other buildings, including the village school, the town hall and the chateau. On the main square, across from the main gates of the chateau, there was a small hotel with a bistro at street level. Along the main street there was a grocery, a bakery, a Catholic church and in the distance, in the open fields, the Georgian Cemetery.

In spite of the presence of these shops the village was not a lively place. Traffic consisted mostly of horse drawn farm vehicles, farm animals and tractors, with the occasional private auto passing through, the streets often ornamented by the dung of cows or horses. No one was ever in any hurry.

## At Madame Brou's

Before the war, my family did not live in the chateau. We would stay at Madame Brou's house, across the way, where we occupied several rooms at ground level, facing a pleasant garden, with a little pond full of water lilies and lazy red fish that were the subject of endless fascination for Anouche and Minouche, the two family cats that accompanied us everywhere for nearly twenty years. This garden, like the other village gardens, extended way back, rising up almost as far as the national highway at the side of the hill. Sometimes, in a fit of boldness, we children would venture out all the way to this highway, where we whiled away the time playing "auto-tennis", a variation on the game of "beard tennis" that was popular at that time. The rules of beard tennis were to walk around the streets of Paris in twos or threes, endeavoring to be the first to spy a bearded man, thus gaining points, as in tennis: 15, 30, 40, advantage gained or lost, and game!

The object of auto-tennis was to be first to announce the make of each car as it appeared in the distance, the winner accruing points just as in beard tennis. I now remember models long disappeared, such as *Delage, Delahaye, Hispano-Suiza, Panhard, Simca, Chénard et Walker* (pronounced like one word: *Shenarivalker*), as well as the more familiar Renault and Citroën. Often we had to wait for as much as ten minutes for a vehicle to come by, and this on a national highway less than twenty kilometers from Paris. How things have changed!

**The Chateau**

Across the road was the chateau, behind a wall of moss-eaten stones pierced by a postern at one end and on the other by a great iron gate which opened onto a road lined with imposing Linden trees. Another postern adjoined the Iron Gate, which was only opened to let in the rare carriage or vehicle. In front of the gate, on the small 011square, a metallic tower several story tall dominated the village. It was said that the tower had been erected for the training of firemen. We never saw a single fireman there, but it was certainly an irresistible attraction for us boy and girls, given that we were forbidden to climb it.

Entering the chateau by way of the iron gate, at left were a group of buildings and sheds, a sort of farm with chicken coop, rabbits and other farm animals, compost shed, and my friend, the dog Lord. All of this constituted the realm of Namo and Valodia Gogouadze. Perhaps realm seems like an overstatement, since they only had one "slave" – well, not a real one, but he sure acted the part: Sebasti worked from dawn to night, hardly ever mixing in with the groups of men discussing the events of the day – the principal occupation of the other residents of the chateau, and in general he remained silent on all occasions. I don't remember ever hearing the sound of his voice.

Continuing down the great lane of linden trees as it bent to the right, you would arrive at the grandly named chateau, a rather undistinguished two-story mansion of yellowish stones with white trim. The façade faced south, toward the valley. On the side with the linden trees a glassed-in belvedere rose above the building, where we children firmly believed that a *Grand-Duc* (Eagle Owl) and other owls had established residence. We never saw a single one.

Behind the chateau and against the retaining wall were some run-down structures which housed the Georgian print shop, some agricultural tools, the Georgian governmental archives until they were finally sent to Harvard University for preservation, and Colonel Tsereteli.

**The Colonel**

Colonel Tsereteli was a retired Georgian officer whose occupation consisted entirely in serving as *Tamada* — toast-master — during the numerous *keipis* (banquets) that took place, lasting often from afternoon until the following dawn. Enormous quantities of red wine were consumed, Colonel Tsereteli breaking all records, as was only proper for a successful Tamada. And with that, he never got drunk.

The colonel's factotum was named Isidore, who was also the printer of the Georgian colony. Whenever something needed to be printed, it was he who worked in our primitive print shop where everything was done manually, like in olden times, housed in a shed adjacent to the colonel's shabby lodgings.

How many *Keipi* were held there over the years! The great table or tables around which thirty or more celebrants could be seated always looked immaculate since tablecloths were disposed of. What a contrast to the colonel's bed: this was a real disaster, sagging and pitiful, and the kitchen was rather barren, yet gave birth to enormous quantities *of lobio, satsivi, kharcho, romi* and other traditional Georgian dishes.

The guests came from Paris, some twenty kilometers away, and they brought the food and drink, since the colonel didn't have a penny. What he had, and what no amount of money could buy, was hospitality, camaraderie and such a big and generous heart that to be near him, even without speaking to him, one would feel enveloped by his warmth. It was undoubtedly for that reason that the banquets were held at his place. Often they would last from Friday to Monday! The guests would come and go, but the colonel remained there, at his place as Tamada, a role that he filled with brilliance and dignity.

One day the colonel got sick, for the first time in his life. The doctor came, and since I happened to be there, I served as interpreter. The colonel was 82 years old at that time, and although he had been in France for thirty years, he could not speak one word of French.

*The doctor*: Ask him if he drinks a lot.

*Me:* Colonel, the doctor wants to know if you drink a lot.

*The Colonel:* Drink? Alcohol? No, I don't drink. I only drink red wine.

*The doctor:* Well, how much does he drink?

*The Colonel:* Oh, I drink a bit here and there, normally.

*The doctor:* But what does he mean, normally? *One* bottle

per day? Three? five?

*The Colonel:* (indignant) What? Five bottles? What does he take me for, a child?

After some more back and forth, the Colonel admitted that now that he was getting on in years, he only drank about eight bottles daily. Hiding his surprise, the doctor prescribed him to limit himself to four bottles. "If I restrict him to any less than that, he will die, his organism is so accustomed to wine!"

**At the Chateau**

We rented from Madame Brou, I believe, because my father didn't want to take possession of living quarters in the chateau for the relatively short time that we would spend in Leuville. During that period, the chateau was occupied by impoverished Georgians who did not have the means to rent elsewhere. Among them were Ephtime Takaishvili, noted archeologist, Samson Pirtskhalava, Nestor Kalandadze, noted humorist, the Uratadze family, and many others.

Then the war came, the chateau emptied out, rooms became available, and it was then that we took possession of two large rooms on the second floor, at the top of the staircase on the left, which dominated the façade, the front garden, the field and the Orge Valley, a small, calm river that ran hidden through the woods. On the opposite slope, some seven kilometers away, one could make out the buildings of the Brétigny railway station.

The sanitary facilities in the chateau were quite primitive. There was no running water at all. Responsibility fell upon me to fetch water at the spring, which was situated under the outer walls. As for the toilets, there was only one in each wing, on the upper or first floor. The one on our side we had to share with everyone, since the other one was located inside the apartment of the Uratadze family, who were permanent residents of the chateau. As there was no running water, therefore no flushing, the used toilet paper, *i.e.* newspaper, was thrown into a large waste bin.

I don't know who it was who emptied it from time to time and burned the contents. It is astonishing for me to think that with those conditions, the toilet really didn't smell so bad, or maybe it was just that we were so used to it that we really didn't even notice.

## We the Children

Yes, Leuville dominates my childhood memories, even though it was Vanves, a middle-class suburb of Paris, that was our year-round home. My best friends weren't the French kids with whom I went to school, even though we were stuck in the same classes year after year. Instead, they were the other Georgian children: the Tsouladze kids, Tamara and Ninouka – but not their brother Serge, the Communist, who was far too mature to mix in with our scampering. There was also Claude Kemoularia, the Zaldastani brothers, Givi and Otar, the last one with his head already steeped in abstruse mathematical ponderings. And then there were Shaliko Sepiskveradze, Kheto Barnovi, Nutsa Ramishvili, Koka Djakeli, Theo and Zeinab Kedia – this one for just a short time, since she married very young and thus becoming a respectable woman, didn't stoop to mix with us — and finally, Medounia Uratadze, my old friend, whom we half in jest called the princess of the chateau, as she was the only one of our crowd who lived there all year round.

All of us grew up together helter-skelter, playing, pulling pranks and getting into mischief. Later on we indulged ourselves in our first flirtations, so light and sweet! These never led to anything serious; we were too much like brothers and sisters.

## The Climber

I must have been around 14 years old when a mania for heights took hold of me. Wherever I was I climbed to the top: ladder, roof, rocks, cliffs, trees; and in Leuville, in addition to the great linden trees of the main alley, there were at the bottom of the garden, growing on the inside edge of the terrace overlooking the apple orchard, three magnificent linden trees with entangled branches, raising their leafy limbs to the sky.

So many hours I spent there, balancing over the chasm! Up there I was the master, I needed no one. Of course when my little friends came with me it was even more fun, daring each other to more audacious feats, betting on who would climb the highest. And the girls would beg us not to be stupid and come down to safety — in vain, of course, since isn't it exhilarating to be entreated by an anxious feminine voice? Nothing more effective to push boys toward the most daring feats!

Even alone I would go there all the time, escorted by Lord, my faithful friend, who was compelled, simple dog that he was, to remain a pedestrian on the ground. I was there so much, high up on these trees, that everybody knew where to find me.

A vivid remembrance comes to me. I was probably 16 years old. I was perched high on a limb, higher than I ever dared; and I was drunk, drunk from the wine I had imbibed at some keipi, drunk from my young immortal strength, drunk from dominating the village of Leuville, the chateau, the valley, the earth, the universes. I must have been behaving even more recklessly than usual, since I saw down below several of my buddies, my mother, sundry adults, their faces turned toward the heavens entreating me to please come down, climb down right away, but not too fast, oh my god, to be careful. And I, show off, perched there singing at the top of my lungs, an unbreakable bird, until I see my father hurrying through the fields, stick in hand; and before he had time to say anything, with horrified groans in counterpoint, I tumble down to say on the ground, angelic: "What's the matter? I was perfectly safe; there is nothing to worry about. " And the day after, there I would be again.

My obsession with heights lasted a long time. When I could it was mountain climbing, but more often it was rocks, cliffs, and above all trees, more trees, again trees … until one day, at age 35, I finally fell, not from very high, in the Fontainebleau forest, a broken branch making me lose my grip, and I smashed my right hip. Never again did that leg function at 100%. That ended my climbing, so I turned to my other love, sailing. But what remained with me was what my colleagues at Yale termed "your attraction to vertical surfaces", which translated thereafter into promenades on hilly trails, cliff paths, and now that I am nearing 90, simple flights of stairs.

## People of the Chateau

In those times the chateau was an entity brimming with life. Many Georgians lived there year-round, composing a lively microcosm reinforced on weekends and holidays by their compatriots coming from Paris or further afield. Several families had settled there, such as the Gogouadze, Eradze, Ouratadze, and also a number of gentlemen, most of them not single by choice but because when they fled Georgia for what they thought would be a temporary exile, wives and children remained behind to be stuck forever.

The chateau proper was so full that quite a few found lodgings outside the property, some in Leuville itself, others in nearby villages such as Longjumeau – known for the years Lenin lived there before World War I – Linas, Monthlery, Arpajon. For all, the social center remained the lawn of the chateau or, in bad weather, the so-called salon, a large room on the ground floor where portraits and photographs of personalities of the first Georgian Republic and other mementos were displayed.

There was no day in which one would not see a half-dozen gentlemen engaged in deep conversation, standing in circles, or proceeding at a deliberate pace, stopping often in order to better emphasize a point of discussion. Often enough that happened with a rake or a hoe on the shoulder, since they had sallied forth with the intention of working their vegetable patch. Intention maybe, but in reality....

I can still see one of these would-be gardeners setting out with his tool in hand:

He steps out on the lawn, looks at the sky, slowly, to make sure of the weather like any real peasant. Disappointed to see that the weather is fine, he slowly proceeds toward his patch, all the time looking around, full of hope — a stop in front of the rhododendrons, another in the main alley, yet another under the linden trees. Nobody in sight? With a heavy step he goes on his way.

But from the corner of his eye he glimpses one of his compatriots who, like himself, had stepped out with a spade on his shoulder. Immediately they wait for each other, get together, and together proceed on their way. They have not made ten steps that they stop in order to better discuss something ... and soon another gentleman appears, then another. Before they realize it morning is gone; noon strikes at the town-hall clock; time for lunch, followed by a siesta— and in the afternoon the whole shebang again....

To be just, I must say that not all were like that: some worked their land very hard. The 20 acres of the property had been divided into plots granted to the inhabitants according to a method that for me remained obscure. A large parcel, the biggest, had devolved to Nametia and Valodia Gogouadze, who were helped in their daily work by their farmhand Sebasti.

### The Farm

They were installed in the outlaying buildings located near the main entrance gate, which they had transformed into a prosperous farm complete with chicken coops, pig sty, rabbit hutches, and barn. No horse, however, and I do not remember ever seeing a tractor or other mechanical device. Everything was done by hand.

Valodia had been a colonel in the Georgian army and from the wounds he had suffered in the course of his duties remained a stiff leg, which he used to flog with live nettles to relieve the rheumatism that afflicted him, to the horror of us children. Together with his farmhand Sebasti, Valodia assumed all the field work, with only occasionally some outside help.

I remember one year he had hired a few village women to help with the raspberry crop, and as they worked he would exhort them: "Sing! Sing!" which they willingly did to help pass the time. But his reason was not the love of song, but rather because if they were singing, they could not stuff themselves with his precious berries!

Nametia, his wife, took full care of the household, the chickens, the rabbits, milking the cows like a typical farmer's wife of the times, without any help. She fabricated a Georgian cheese, Suluguni, the only place where it could be found in all of France, and naturally cooked typical Georgian dishes such as Lobia, Satsivi, Kharcho, Pkhali, Kachapuri, and more. She would also prepare dishes with a corn flour basis, Tchadi and Romi, similar to the italian Polenta. But corn flour could not be found anywhere in France – corn was considered just good enough for cattle – so that she would grind it herself in a kind of large coffee grinder, by hand of course.

How comfortable it felt, how good it smelled in the Gogouadze's great room, a space which served as kitchen, dining room, living room, and even bedroom in winter. The large coal cooking stove was always lit, on which all day long various dishes simmered and of course a tea kettle, since tea was drunk at all times. Under the stove, or rather in the lower drawer, where pans and lids are usually kept, Nametia had made a sort of rag nest where all year round would snooze a mother cat and her kittens.

At noon and at seven at night one could hear throughout the property the sound of the triangle with which she would call her men for meals. Few were the times when there were not a half-dozen persons at the table, often more, without counting us the children, for whom she always had some kind of treat.

Active, hard-working, sociable, generous, the Gogouadze remained one of the pillars of the chateau until Nametia died at age 97, around 1986, active to the end. Valodia had passed away some 15 years earlier. All through her life Nametia was surrounded by celibate gentlemen who spent holidays and weekends at the farm. When they got older and retired, a few of them settled there permanently, keeping her company until they also disappeared from this world.

**The Eradze**

Another hard-working couple comes to mind: Mr. and Mrs. Eradze. He had been Agriculture Minister during my father's presidency; thus, it seemed fitting that they would become full-time farmers in exile. They had been allocated a sizable portion of the land that they worked with a relentless determination; yet their life-style was quite different from that of the Gogouadze.

Mrs. Eradze, who was Russian, was very reserved, spoke little, did not seem to have any friends, and no one ever visited her. As for me, if sometimes my mother would send me to their lodgings for an errand, I was always impatient to get out of there, because it was dark, smelled of humidity, of stale air, of rancid old person —perhaps because Mrs. Eradze's mother, who never set foot outside, was always there in an armchair near the window, her shriveled face peering out from under the mounds of blankets and shawls under which she was buried.

As for Mr. Eradze, he would occasionally join the groups discussing on the lawn, but never for very long, except on Sundays where he would allow himself not to work in the fields all day long. He was well esteemed but at a distance. My mother respected him enormously, and I now know they had deep feelings for each other.

When my mother reached 85 years of age, Mrs. Eradze died. Her husband was then perhaps 87. My father had passed away some 10 years before. Thus, finally, after having known and appreciated each other for more than a half-century, Mr. Eradze and my mother could share a little intimacy.

*My Mother at 89*

## Poor Data

And then there was Data. Stocky, dark complexion, drooping mustache, heavy in mind and body, he relentlessly worked his plot of land located outside the chateau, where he lived in a sort of dilapidated cabin. He owned a delivery tricycle with which he painfully transported his produce to the Paris markets, an exhausting journey especially for him who was well past middle-age.

One fall day, alerted by desperate cries, we rushed to the lawn: it was Data, bellowing his despair, tearing mustache and hair, in short in a frightful state. To our questions he would only answer, between his sobs: "Stove! My Stove! I lit my stove...!" With great difficulty we managed to calm him, and he finally could tell us what had happened:

That morning, for the first time since spring, the weather turned cold, so that he lit his stove, already stuffed with old newspapers and kindling. A few minutes later, after he had added some coal and waited for it to take, he remembered that he had hidden in the stove, under newspapers and kindling, week after week, all the money he had earned during the growing season, money that had just been transformed into smoke, that poor money that cost him so much work and upon which he counted to survive the winter!

Poor Data! Not only was he left with nothing, but when he confessed his tale of sorrow everybody burst out laughing, making fun of him: How could anyone be so stupid? Who ever heard of hiding banknotes in a stove? And banks, he never heard of them? Saving accounts?

After that first reaction, however, the Georgians collected some money to help him through the winter, but for a long time it was enough for someone to pretend lighting a stove for all to burst out laughing.

What a panorama of human diversity in the social microcosm contained in the chateau! The colonel, the former minister, simple Data, all worked hard but with very different styles and results: the latter always overwhelmed, always on the brink of utter destitution; the Eradze, withdrawn and apart, living poorly, lacking everything, asking nothing from anybody; and the Gogouadze, generous in their gregarious prosperity, warmly surrounded by a circle of compatriots in a friendship that never faltered. In the old country they would have certainly become Kulaks.

---

# 7. Matter and Mind

**Money Questions**

As is natural for children, the question of how and with what kind of income we managed didn't in the slightest preoccupy me. It was only well after that time that I looked back, and from snatches of conversation I overheard here and there I was able to reconstitute that part of our history. Following the treaty of Brest-Litovsk, when the Bolsheviks made peace with the Germans in 1917, a great number of Polish soldiers who had been forcibly inducted into the Tsarist armies were left practically abandoned on the frontier between Georgia and Turkey. The Russian generals had been extremely wary of the Polish recruits and had sent them to the Turkish front – (Turkey was Germany's ally) — where they didn't run the risk of finding themselves face to face with so-called enemies who were themselves Polish as well. Reason being, Poles had also been drafted into the Kaiser's armies, since at that time Poland was divided between Germany and Russia.

In 1918, when Georgia declared its independence, it signed a treaty with the newly reconstituted Polish state by which the Georgian authorities took charge of the repatriation of these Polish soldiers in return for gradual repayment of the associated expenses. Then, in 1921 Georgia was invaded by the Red Army. Poland, refusing to recognize the USSR and considering Georgia's legal government to be my father's government-in-exile, continued its payment to the Georgian legation in Paris. This went on until 1939, when Poland was again divided between Germany and the Soviet Union, temporarily ceasing to exist as a nation except for its Government-in-exile in London. The money paid by the Poles until that time was used to finance the Georgian government's activities, and to assure its leaders a meager pension.

That pension was indeed quite modest: I don't believe my father bought a suit during all his time in exile! And I well remember that until his death in 1953 he was wearing the same great-coat, patched a hundred times, that he had brought with him from Georgia. In 1952, when I was working at United Press International, my boss, Ed Korry, made me a gift of three brand-new suits he had ordered from the States and which turned out to be too small by the time he received them: oh the good French cuisine! One of those fit my father perfectly, the first new suit I remember him in. And it is in that Brook Brothers suit that he was buried.

When the war came and Poland collapsed in 1939, the payments ceased. If I understand correctly, the Georgian émigrés who were members of the Social-Democrat Party contributed to the living expenses of their President. That was easy during the war, since quite a few Georgians made a lot of money in the black market, as, incidentally, did a great many Frenchmen. But my father would accept only the minimum he needed to live, and in addition was quite discriminating. He always scrutinized the list of would-be contributors and rejected all those he deemed unsuitable for political or other reasons. One of those contributors remains in memory: Mr.Leon Eligulashvili, who represented the Jewish Georgians who had settled in France (In this year 2011, he is still with us and in good shape at the young age of 105!).

The reason I remember him particularly has nothing to do with politics: It is because he faithfully brought a huge stack of Matza on each of his visits, of which I became inordinately fond! Georgians and Georgian Jews always got along very well. Perhaps it is because Georgians always considered them first Georgians, and Jews only second. In keeping with the age-old Georgian tradition, my father and his associates managed to convince the Nazi authorities that this was an historical and genetic fact (that the Georgian Jews were Georgians first and foremost) with the consequence that throughout the war not a single Georgian Jew was ever molested in any way.

After the war, with all the hopes of a return to Georgia destroyed by the German defeat, yet at the same time my parents' belief in democracy renewed by this same defeat, our household situation became even more difficult. The lack of money became ever more evident. Despite that, my father refused all proposals of a political nature, notably that made by the United States, which wanted to bring him to Washington as an advisor to the State Department. "If I accept this proposal," he said, "I will lose my freedom to act. Instead of thinking one hundred percent for Georgia and acting in its best interest, automatically and with the best intentions in the world I would think partially in terms of the United States."

When he died in 1953 just before turning 85, the Georgians offered a pension to my mother, who was 75. She flatly refused. "I am not Noé, you don't owe me anything, especially since you don't have much yourselves. I thank you with all my heart, but no. I'll manage by myself." And she did manage, owing nothing to anyone, with the help of the small pension the French government granted to all seniors citizens.

When I learned much later of rumors circulating in certain émigré circles, as well as in Soviet Georgia, concerning a national treasure that my father was alleged to have taken with him and on which he lived in opulence, I could only laugh. I know all too well that this supposed national treasure of gold and silver was never more than the fruit of malevolent imaginations.

### Noé's Death

From 1925 on we lived at No.11 Solférino Street in Vanves, a suburb to the South of Paris, close to the Porte de Versailles. It was a two-story row house with façade on the street and a small garden in the back. That's where I spent my school-age, student, war years. That's where Noé died of a lightning heart attack in January 1953, that's where his wife

Ina Ivanovna died in 1967.

Now, in the year 2000, there are two subway stops nearby. But in those times the house in Vanves was not of easy access: the closest subway stop was Porte de Versailles, a good 20 minutes brisk walk away. There was a slow shuttle bus from the subway stop, but the service was infrequent and stopped completely at 9 p.m. This difficulty of access didn't bother Noé, who seldom went to Paris proper and would mostly stay at home, where day after day he received many visitors, as we have seen.

But after the war, with the victory of the Allies and the strengthening of Stalin's empire, any hope that Georgia would again become free and independent disappeared. My father nevertheless continued with his struggle against Bolshevism, but with the political realities in play the inconveniences of the Vanves house location became apparent: the flow of visitors diminished a lot, in part because my father's friends and contemporaries were getting older and it became more difficult for them to move around.

The daily routine didn't change much, however. Noé kept taking his two daily walks, morning and afternoon. In winter he particularly liked to go to the local cemetery, less than half a mile away, where he had found a stone bench in a corner, protected from the wind, which concentrated the  sun rays. Thus it is that responding to his implicit wish his grave was first established in that very corner of the Vanves cemetery. Only after my mother's death some 15 years later was his coffin transferred to a family vault in the Georgian cemetery of Leuville. Now, in 2011 that vault shelters Noé, First President of the Georgian Republic, his wife Ina Korenevna, his daughter Asmath, and his son-in-law Levan Pagava.

My father often told us, as he was getting older, that he would not reach his 85th birthday. "In my family," he would say, "no male has lived to that age." Concerned about his health, nevertheless, he read works like "*How to Live to a*

*Hundred,"* amassing practical advice and visions of the future, he led a very healthy life and continued to the very end in full possession of his physical and mental faculties, except for a little shriveling and a slight loss of hearing — he even had all his teeth! Despite all that, one must believe, he had so thoroughly convinced himself that he would not see 85 that he died suddenly in the night just a week before his 85th birthday!

If one needs more to confirm the power of mind over flesh, let us reflect that in order to attain this particular result, he had to perform impressive mental gymnastics: he was born on January 2, old style, and died on January 7 of our calendar, which would have been December 26 old style! In other words, he had to take into account this calendar shift to succeed in dying before he turned 85!

Note that to this day the religious Orthodox calendar, which was also the secular norm under the Tsars remains, 13 days behind ours, since the Orthodox Church never accepted the Papal reform under which the Western Catholic nations jumped thirteen days in 1582 in order to make dates coincide with seasons and religious holidays based on astronomical events. This is why the Bolshevik October Revolution was traditionally celebrated November 7.

A short time before his death Noé had finished writing his memoirs, *My Past*, which our ancient Georgian printing shop in Leuville had been in the process of publishing. They pressed with the work faster than usual in order to bring it out as a surprise at my father's birthday. The book was ready two weeks early, printed, bound, and cut. Alas, he never saw it, and the first numbered copy was buried with him. As for me, what I regret the most is that he did not live a little longer, enough to witness the death of Stalin, which occurred a few months later.

Still it is passing strange that Noé should die at that date only so as not to fall afoul of the family tradition and not reach his 85th birthday — which tends to underline the superiority of the mental over the physical — and not only during life, as we shall see below in the case of my sister Atia. But more on Noé…

The day of Noé's funeral a rather unforeseen crowd of several thousand persons invaded the rue Solférino, spilling over to adjoining streets. So much so that Vanves' mayor decided that it was imperative to make an exception to the rule that a funeral had to proceed by the shortest way from the place where the coffin was located to the burial site. "There are so many people, he exclaimed, that if we go straight to the cemetery most people will still be on rue Solférino!" And so, with the help of additional police, the cortege was routed in a roundabout way to the cemetery where the funeral service took place.

President Noé Jordania's funeral, as well as the numerous newspaper articles and editorials that it occasioned, clearly demonstrated that although he had been somewhat neglected in his last years, he nevertheless represented a fundamental slice of history not only in what concerned Georgia, but also for 20th century history of socialism and the evolution of modern societies. His political and social philosophy remains of a vivid actuality, as is everyday demonstrated by the essential place that policies based on enlightened socialism occupy in the world.

---

*From: Editorial, The New York Times*
*Thursday, January 15, 1953, page 36*

## DEATH OF A PRESIDENT

The death of Noah Jordania in Paris comes little more than three decades after the military overthrow by Soviet troops of the independent Georgian republic of which M. Jordania was the first and only president. In the years from 1918 to 1921 M. Jordania and his associates tried to create a democratic republic with moderate leaders who looked to the United States and its Constitution for their model.

Viewed superficially, the efforts of M. Jordania and his contemporaries in other lands were failures. But they made a page of history, which has not been forgotten and one that retains relevance for any consideration of how the peoples of the present Soviet Union may live together in the future when their present tyrannical rule has become a memory.

———————

## My Sister Atia

It is now some thirty years later. My sister Atia is about to give her soul to the hereafter, that beautiful soul that had been for so long the conscience of the Georgian colony in Paris. In the hospital a priest is making his rounds, fulfilling his priestly mission. He comes to my sister's bed, and, after the usual platitudes, he asks her: "My daughter, do you believe in God?" And my sister, with the frank and direct language so characteristic of her, answers with decision: "Yes, I am a believer, but I need no intermediary!"

The titular priest of the Georgian parish was father Melia. He had held that position for many years, fulfilled faithfully his duties, visiting Georgian families, comforting the bereaved, performing marriages, baptisms, funerals. Yet my sister didn't like him, neither as a priest nor as a man. "He looks so prim, so unctuous, that I can't stand him. He is, at bottom, unsound," she'd say. And she often stated that when she died, she did not want any religious service, and above all did not want Father Melia to officiate.

Then she died. Giving in to the pressures of the Georgian colony, to customs, to conformism, the family decided that there would be a service in the Leuville church, near where the Georgian cemetery is located. I was still in New York the day she died, but I was able to arrive in time for the ceremony.

That Sunday it was raining hard, which it rarely did. The rain was coming down in buckets, starting early in the morning. Despite it all the church was packed. It was the Catholic Church, as there is no Orthodox church in Leuville; everyone was seated, with our family in the first row. Father Melia — yes, it was he who officiated — was doing what priests do on such occasions. Reciting the Orthodox ritual, he roamed around the casket which was placed — I was going to say on stage — in front of the altar, swinging with one hand the censer at the end of its chains, from which clouds of incense escaped, purposefully directed in turn towards the audience, the four cardinal points, and above all towards the coffin: from in front; from behind; from each side … and all of a sudden, at the top of a swing, the censer explodes! There is no other word: it explodes, as if a bullet had squarely hit! Pieces fall every which way, the incense scatters on the floor where it continues to burn … Father Melia, thunderstruck, stands frozen, the chain dangling bereft from his hand….

And Levan, Atia's husband, with a happy chuckle says: "Here she is, Atia, she is right here with us!" And all of us, husband, children, brother, sister, friends, we all feel our heavy hearts becoming lighter and cheerier by knowing she is so close and letting us know that she disapproves.

Several years later, meeting Father Melia in New York, I reminded him of this episode. He looked at me straight in the eyes and retorted in an icy voice: "I do not remember."

-----

# 8. Georgians

## Shota

It was around 1930 that Shota appeared in my young life. One of my father's associates, Noe Ramishvili, who had been Interior Minister in his cabinet, had been murdered by an agent of the KGB. Because of that the Georgians decided that my father needed a bodyguard; and it was Shota Kartsivadze who was chosen. He came to us as a bodyguard, but he soon became much more: a family friend giving a helping hand at any occasion, doing small errands, cultivating the vegetable garden, even giving me my bath on occasion.

He was sturdily build, of a dark complexion, with a small moustache, and always carried his gun in his back pocket. Occasionally he would allow me to hold it in my eager hands, after having carefully removed the magazine and verified that no bullet remained in the breech. He even let me fire it sometimes on an improvised target in the basement.

Shota would appear at eight in the morning, since he insisted on bringing my father his breakfast tray. Then at eleven, when my father went for his walk, he would escort him, walking a couple of paces behind and on the side. Wherever my father went, Shota would of course be with him. Upon reflection, as a bodyguard he could not have been terribly effective. It would have been so easy for anyone to fool his meager defenses, given my father's regular habits, or to operate between the hours of 7 at night and 8 in the morning, when was back home. One must believe Shota was there for the principle, rather than for any real action. As for me, going back to these far-away times, I can only rejoice for his long presence, since my father, affable, receiving everybody, almost always home, nevertheless remained somewhat of an abstraction in his ivory tower; and despite his

113

continuous presence, these everyday family lunches and dinners, he remained at a remove.

I hardly remember any discussion, advice, or directive. He was rather like a patriarch, distant although present, who somehow determined lines of action, ways of behavior, limits to respect, without ever establishing these rules directly. Perhaps it was like these theoreticians of abstract mathematics understood by only a handful of scientists, whose task is to explain the mysteries to the rest of the world. Thus my father's thoughts were conveyed to me by others, Shota mainly, without speeches or sermonizing dictates, but rather through everyday words, remarks, anecdotes, tales of the Georgia that remain for him so close yet to me appeared so faraway, a legendary realm.

Rather illogically, when World War II was declared in 1939, it was decided that a bodyguard had become unnecessary. Shota by then was much too old to enlist, like many Georgians did—on the side of the Germans in order to help destroy the Soviet Union and free Georgia from the communist yoke. I think he tried to make a living in the black market, without great success, as he was much too honest. But during that time he made it his business to come visit us often – he lived in the neighborhood – bringing small gifts of foodstuff, which were so welcome in those times of scarcity. And it was for me every time a source of calm satisfaction to see him faithful to himself, now treating me as the man I had not yet quite become.

**Visitors**

So many visitors day after day! Some were regulars, companions of the struggle for independence, old comrades of the nationalist trenches who would come to father to discuss the political questions of the times, particularly how that could affect Georgia's future. They would talk at great length, often coming up with the most romantically impractical suggestions, far-fetched ideas to which my father would patiently listen – at least that's what Shota would tell me. As for me, I had not the slightest interest in those questions that were so far-removed from my youthful preoccupations. It is only later that I understood that these conversations had some practical *raison d'être*. They allowed the Georgians in exile frequent contact with their President, through which they reaffirmed themselves, reinforced their warm tribal feelings of belonging that allowed them to retain their Georgian identity and differentiate themselves from the Parisian masses that could so easily smother their sense of belonging to the far-off homeland.

**Gentlemen of the Government**

Some visitors had their regular days and times, mostly those who had been members of my father's cabinet and who, rather pathetically, still considered themselves thus even twenty years later. To my young eyes they were the most important persons in the world, these imposing men who seemed to carry in their person the whole of Georgia, center of their world, the weight of the universe, the connection to the years bygone and the decisions to come. And they came all the way to our house, they gathered around my father, they deferred to him!

There was Mister Akaki Chengeli, who had been Prime Minister. Massive and heavy, comfortably dressed, with an interested and kindly expression, he contrasted with his wife Makriné, small and slender, with wide-open eyes under her tortoise-shell glasses with thick lenses, since she was as short-sighted as a mole.

There was Evgeni Gegechkori, tall and well built, always elegant with his signature bow-ties that contrasted with his colleagues ordinary neck adornments, and who gave the impression of being privy to international secrets and in cahoots with the most exalted authorities.

Mr. Kandelaki tended to the reddish with his rust-colored beard, his brownish suit – probably the only one he owned –

and his big shell-colored glasses. Tchichiko Assatiani sticks in my memory with his goatee and drooping mustache, and because my mother called him by his name and patronymic, rather hilarious to my ears: Sosepath Samsonovitch.

And there were many others I remember indistinctly, such as the afore mentioned Noe Ramishvili who was murdered when I was 10 years old, Noe Tsintsadze who owned a small yoghurt factory located in the Marais section of Paris, a certain Valiko that we the children, I don't know why, had nicknamed Valicon (Vali-the-stupid); there was also Sandro Menagari, a close family friend, who at the start of WWII left for Istanbul with his Polish wife, where he settled as a pig farmer, a cover for his clandestine activities as a contact for Georgian patriots in Georgia proper — at least that was what I was led to understand later. I remember that when I was small, he would take me hoeing with him in the garden, where he managed to make me find bronze pennies in the overturned soil, which he told me were excreted by the worms — I clung to that belief for a long time.

Well, when all these important men were gathered, it was enough for my father to just appear—tall, slender, white hair and beard, indifferently dressed—for it to become immediately apparent who was the boss. He never failed to dominate any assembly, even before saying a word.

And that's how he remains in my memory: a dominant presence, a powerful personality, in a word: a leader, without any possible doubt.

**Vlasa**

Some Georgians would appear at infrequent intervals, mainly those who lived in the provinces or abroad, while others were practically everyday regulars. And as for me, a brash spoiled kid, I would sometimes behave towards them in such a cheeky, shameless manner that when I recall my actions I feel like slapping myself.

I am thinking particularly of Vlasa Mgeladzé, an old revolutionary with a tinge of terrorism, who never ceased to fascinate me, whom I greatly admired, and whom at the same time I used to tease shamelessly.

A handsome, powerful man, very strong even in his old age, Vlasa had the particularity that he had lost the thumb of his left hand together with several finger joints. It was rumored that during the revolutionary struggle against the tsarist regime his specialty was to fabricate bombs and that one had exploded in his hands, with that result. He was also celebrated for his exploits against the Okrana, the tsar's secret police. Of all these feats I remember only one:

Arrested in Budapest – how? why? – the police had handcuffed him with his hands behind his back. They were bringing him to headquarters in a horse carriage, a policeman on either side, another next to the coachman, and two behind. They had not noticed that he was missing a thumb, or thought nothing of it. So that, as the coach was crossing a bridge over the Danube, Vlasa managed to slide his hands free from the handcuffs, grabbed his guards on either side by the neck, stunned them by banging their heads together and, before the policemen had time to react, jumped off and dove into the river swollen by the melting snows.

Immediately a hue and cry followed with the search concentrated down river since the current was very violent. But Vlasa, thanks to his Herculean strength, had managed to swim up-river and to hide behind one of the bridges' pillars for several hours, until night fell and the search was abandoned. He then let the current bring him to the shore down river, which he managed to scale more dead than alive.

"And then?" we would ask, panting.

"Oh then I undressed, squeezed the water out my clothes, put them back on, still very cold but at least not dripping, and went to find refuge with one of my lady friends, who comforted and warmed me in a very personal way." And with these memories a far-away look of longing would come over him, while my sister and I looked at him open-mouthed, never imagining what that "personal way" could mean.

Well, this powerful man, this hero, this magnificent orator who was always in great demand to deliver the eulogy customary to any funeral, this man, then, we made him the butt of a nasty, repeated prank. One of his characteristic traits was a leonine profile with a thick mane of hair combed to the back. I cannot remember which of us, my sister or I, had invented this cruel game, by which we would sneak behind him, unaware, and all of a sudden sweep his hair backwards, to his face, while yelling in his ear "Why not like that!" and then flee at full speed, giggling uncontrollably. And this not once in a while, but several succeeding times, taking advantage, I later understood, of his deficient hearing to surprise him repeatedly.

And this powerful man who with the flick of a finger could have thrown us across the room, he contented himself to comb his hair back with his hand, pronouncing a few indistinct words, but never saying anything to our parents who would undoubtedly have punished us severely.

I don't know how long we indulged in this cruel game. I hope it didn't last too long. In any case it remains in my memory like a slice of life, Vlasa always alive, massive and kindly then as now.

**Thina**

Another frequent visitor was Ceo Sardjveladze, the father of my buddy Thina, whose pre-matrimonial adventure is worth recounting. How naïve could we be!

Ceo owned a yogurt factory in Malakof near our house in Vanves, so we would see each other often, Thina and I, particularly when we were older and reached the age to go to the Quartier Latin, the Sorbonne area on the left bank.

## Georgians

It was during the war. The Germans occupied Paris and three-quarters of France. The part which was not occupied was ruled from Vichy by the collaborationists Laval and Petain. In our Georgian colony where everybody knew everybody forever a new element appeared: freed Georgian prisoners of war. These Georgians were soldiers in the Soviet army made prisoners by the Germans, who granted to some of their non-Russian captives the possibility to enlist in some special units under their command rather than rot away in a concentration camp – which, for those "inferior" races like the Russians, were not much better than a death camp.

It was very natural that many of these young men enlisted thus, even more so because the Georgians had always resented the Russian Soviet hegemony. These units were not displayed on the Eastern front, since the Germans were mistrustful of a possible fraternization, but on the West, guarding the famous Wall of the Atlantic that fell rather promptly when the Allied invaded Normandy.

But coming back to our prisoners: Those who could prove having relatives, even distant, in France could obtain their freedom after some relatively simple formalities. And this is how we witnessed the arrival of a good number of these fellows, most between 20 and 30 years old, who caused many hearts to beat hard among our Georgian young women. Incidentally, coming from the Soviet Union where "blat" was the norm, without speaking a word of French these young men immediately started dealing in the black market and filling their pockets, while so many of us, myself included, watched them operating, flabbergasted and without a penny to our name.

One of them, Leo, fell in love with Thina, who in no way returned the feeling. She had just discovered the Boul'Mich', the student quarter on the Left Bank, where we would often meet, chatting, strolling, sitting in cafes, attending impromptu surprise-parties. Neither she nor I were very conscious of politics, apart from a hate of the Nazis and the Germans in general. We were forgetful of the war, the occupation, which apart from material questions – we were all in a perpetual state of undernourishment – did not weigh much on our student Paris. At most we would see here and there a *feldgrau* uniform that everybody ignored.

One day Thina came to me all upset: "Leo asked my father for my hand, and he gave it!" She was crying bitterly, asking herself, asking me how to escape this fate that seemed to her "worse than death" – as they say in penny romances. It did not occur to her that she could simply refuse: "My father would kill me!" she would exclaim. One must think that in our colony old-fashioned patriarchal mores were strongly embedded, since it didn't occur to me either that it was possible to say no.

Enters Olivier, one of my buddies I met at Langues O', the School of Oriental Languages where I can't remember why we were both studying Turkish. Tall, over six-foot-six, thin, tortoise-shell spectacles, a perpetual cigarette hanging from the corner of his lips, like us he was somewhat lost in this war-time Paris, feeling without being able to articulate it that absurdity of life that soon after Albert Camus would bring to the conscience. Thus we were all three confronting the problem: how to help Thina escape the awful fate that awaited her.

This all was happening at a time when Olivier and I were trying to formulate a plan to escape from Paris, cross clandestinely the demarcation line into non-occupied France, and reach the Cote d'Azur in order to … The rest remained vague, undefined. In any case the pretext had come to push ahead with the project. The only difference was that we would leave together, the three of us.

To cross the demarcation line was not easy without the proper documentation. First we would have to get into the restricted border zone, about 20-kilometers wide, for which a permit was compulsory, that we had no idea how to obtain. Then we would have to cross the border itself, heavily guarded on one side by the Germans and the other the Vichy border patrols. Once on the other side, we thought all would be well, not realizing there would be many police checks, which would not have failed to catch us, since we had no papers for the free zone.

But never you mind. We managed to get some money (How? I can't remember.) We found out what we thought would be the most practical place where to cross, got the name of a "mule". Then, at the last moment, it occurred to us that if we left all three together, Thina's father Ceo would immediately understand what had happened, would alert the authorities, and we would be caught before even reaching the zone. In those times young people, and particularly girls, were expected to be home by 10 at the latest, so that we would have practically no head-start if we did not hide our plans better. Since he did not even suspect Olivier's existence, we decided that I would remain behind to play interference, that after a few days they would let me know where they were, and that I would then join them.

So one nice spring day Olivier and Thina left Paris by train. Early the following day I heard Ceo's voice. He was speaking on the phone: "Yes, my daughter ran away. She's only 17; we must catch her, bring her back. Even worse is that she left with our President's son. I would never have thought he would do such a thing," and so forth.

At that point I came into the room. Ceo was flabbergasted. "I was sure you left with her ... I can see I was wrong ..." and offered his apologies. But still suspicious: "You are her best friend. Are you sure you know nothing?" I played innocent.

A few days went by. Ceo had alerted friends, the colony, the police. I waited for news to know what to do, where to go. Finally a phone call: "I am calling for Olivier. He wants me to tell you he is in the House of Detention of X – a town on the border –, that his friend is also there in the women's wing, that you must do everything to free them, if not they could be

121

there for a long time." And the caller explained he had been in the same prison for attempting to cross the border, and that he spent four months there.

Four months! I didn't have to think long. Alone, without money, I couldn't do anything. It was hard, but I went to see Ceo, told him the news, and confessed everything. Of course he first got furious, then calmed down and managed to get the proper papers to get into the restricted zone. We took the train, arrived in X, immediately went to the House of Detention located downtown, all prepped up for a fight with the prison authorities to free our people.

There we are, at the prison. The gate is wide open on a courtyard, and the first thing that strikes my eye, before even walking in, is a group of people talking with Olivier towering over all, Thina next to him.

We call out, they run to us, Thina jumps to her father's neck, who is much too overcome by emotion to reprimand her, and takes us for a festive meal much appreciated by our jailbirds, since the food in prison was very skimpy indeed. And they recounted what happened, which was a great nothing:

"We arrived by train just like you, and as we got off, right there on the platform, we were picked up by the police: 'No valid documents?' Straight to jail, separated! I sent you a message, I see you got it. And this morning, just like that, I was let go, and in the courtyard I find Thina who was also let go, less than one hour before your arrival." Serendipity indeed!

So we go back to Paris, crestfallen but relieved. Now Thina accepts her fate. Without enthusiasm. But after all Leo is a handsome young man, he does very well in his black market dealings, and back in Georgia his family is well placed within the Soviet system – at least that's what he says. And it still does not occur to Thina that she could simply say no.

The big day is upon us. I have in front of me a wedding photo with Thina in her wedding gown, Leo, myself, friends, family, and behind, towering over everybody, Olivier, cigarette in the corner of his mouth, in his characteristic attitude of the head thrown back so that the smoke would not get in his eyes. [That was probably the last time I saw him: soon after he was caught by the compulsory program of Workers in Germany, sent somewhere East, and disappeared]

The wedding came to a close. Until the last moment Thina was clinging to us, her buddies, her friends, apprehensive yet smiling, but with a kind of unhappy, wan smile: it was clear that this marriage was costing her; but then followed a complete turn-around that I could not fathom, that astounded me, and that I understood only much later.

As soon as the newlyweds came back from a short honeymoon we went to see Thina. What a change! While just a few days before she could hardly stand being close to Leo, barely polite to him, now he seemed to be everything for her. She was constantly next to him, touching him, holding his hand, her eyes fastened on him whatever he was doing. As for us, her buddies, who had been everything to her, it was as if we did not exist. We could just as well be on the moon, the way she ignored us. We tried several times to re-establish the close relationship, but nothing doing. After a while we no longer tried to make contact. I believe she did not even notice.

Later I happened to meet her here and there by chance, but the feeling of friendship was gone. Even later I learned that with Leo and her little daughter Leila they had left for the Soviet Union, that Leo had been arrested as soon as they arrived and sent to a concentration camp in Siberia. And then, nothing.

Almost 45 years later, in 1990, I arrived for the first time in Tbilisi. I managed to find Thina, who had settled in Georgia years before … and our warm relationship resumed as if we had been together only yesterday. Goes to show!

# 9. My Adventures

## Alienation

I was 12 years old when the League of Nations recognized the USSR in its actual borders, in effect recognizing the annexation of Georgia by Russia, and was struggling with my own anguishes, my own crisis, which became acute in that period: revolts, running away, playing hooky — all actions upon which I am sure the rising of the sap was not without influence. As for the political events so discouraging for my parents, I paid no attention to them; even if I had, I probably would not have understood what they were all about. These events didn't seem to affect me, at least not outwardly. Yet I now wonder if, in an indirect way, the deep upheavals of my parents' emotional and political lives didn't influence me by sneakily undermining the basis of the society in which I was growing up. It may well be that my anti-family and anti-social behavior during these times was partially due, in addition to my own problems, to my reaction to a difficult political situation I could feel, even if I had no conscience of it.

My parents did notice, however, that something was amiss with me and tried to do something about it. I remember my mother bringing me to a psychology clinic, where a bald young man in a white coat started asking me questions. I don't think anyone in those times had a good understanding of psychological methods and the difficulty for the practitioner to win trust from his patient, particularly a child. First of all, it did not occur to that young man that he should speak with me privately. My mother was very much there, listening to it all, and I well knew even then that there was no way I could say what was really troubling me in front of her, even if I had been able to express it. Then, as we, or rather I was talking, someone came interrupting, and my psychologist said: "Not

right now, I am busy talking with this boy. It is very amus...."
Then he caught himself and finished: "... very interesting."
But that did it. I closed my mind, stopped talking, and hid
from myself and others for a half century.

## Me, Canadian

What combination of alienation, romanticism, bookish
influences led me to declare to my classmates that I was
Canadian? I must have been less than 12 years old, since this
occurred when I was in grammar school. My best friend and
protector was named Laska, as I recall. We were in the same
class, although he was two years older than me and therefore
much stronger. I can still see him, reddish-hued, pimply faced,
flat haired, with a navy-blue cape flying in the wind, short
pants, beret, and heavy boots of the kind we used to call "shit
stumpers." His cape was always flying, since I see him in full
action, running to my help to drive off the bullies. At the time
I was called by my nickname "Redic," which set me apart
from all the Jean, Michel, Pierre, Paul, Joseph — not much
imagination, those French! [Much later I learned that every
newborn French child was obliged by law to have at least one
name taken from the calendar of Saints.] Naturally my little
friends teased me for my name, calling me "Radish," "Black
Radish," "Ras-du-cul," and other variations. As for Redjeb, my
official name, it would have been even more difficult to bear.

One of my classmate's most frequent questions was:
"What does he do, your father?" to which I answered proudly:
"He's President." To me, and to all the Georgians in exile who
kept drilling it into me, he was in fact still President. "Oh là là,
you're giving us a hard time, stop kidding around...You're
trying to show off, huh?" Among all these sons of tradesmen,
clerks, factory workers, I must indeed have seemed an
arrogant showoff.

Another crime: While not an exceptional student, I loved
to read, and never, never did I talk about sports! Even today I
see no interest in it. That also set me apart from the others who

only read unwillingly and when obliged, and whose horizons consisted of food, home, school, and sports reduced to soccer, basketball, and cycling. I most certainly participated in sports, especially basketball, since I was tall for my age, and I liked it very much. Later I went mountain climbing, sailing, played tennis and even squash. Doing it is fun. Talking about it: what a bore!

But I digress: I had declared myself to be Canadian. That must have been at the period when I read *White Fang, The Long Rifle, The Call of the North,* and other adventure novels about the arctic, which influenced even my ignorant classmates. They knew I wasn't French, so why not be Canadian, which represented adventure and glory? Canada was a land they could relate to, because in addition to the novels, our history classes had filled our heads with the exploits of Jacques Cartier, Jean Bart, Samuel de Champlain, and other glorious French adventurers and pirates. The funniest thing about my imaginary nationality was that my classmates accepted it very quickly, and once I had established myself in a well-defined niche I was never teased again during the remainder of my time at grammar school.

After the *Certificat d'Etudes* (graduation), I don't think I ever saw my classmates again, not even Laska. Well, I did see him maybe once, some months later, when I returned his most prized possession which he had trustfully lent me with his simple faithful soul: *The Red Pirate* in two magnificent volumes bound in a gold cover. Just to look at these books was to share the riches that each pirate owes to himself to conquer!

No, I didn't see them again, my little classmates, since I went on to high school at the Lycée Michelet, while they did not. At the time school was mandatory only up to the age of twelve, so it was usual for parents to put their children into apprenticeship as soon as it was officially allowed: One less mouth to feed, or at least to feed free.

## My Brother Andreika

Why had I declared myself to be Canadian? I now think that in addition to wanting to be accepted at school, I also wanted to escape my emotional and political condition. What a big word, "political," for a child of ten or eleven, you might say. But the term is appropriate. I had had a brother whom I never knew. His name was Andreika, and he died from an accident at the age of twelve. This was a very hard blow to my parents, especially my father, I think. I mentioned before how it was probably thanks to Andreika that I was born: he told my parents he wanted a little brother, and that little brother should be named Redjeb, after a great-grandfather he admired. Thus I came to be born in Paris in 1921, having been conceived, if I am not mistaken, on board the steamship that carried my parents into exile, fleeing from the Soviet armies, which had invaded Georgia. When I was born, my mother was already 45 years old, a late age for a woman to bear children. That is why I am convinced I am the result of parental efforts to replace the son they had lost.

Lost, perhaps, but Andreika's absence weighed heavily on my childhood. After his death, my father had a life-sized marble bust of him made and placed on a high, hollow pedestal, which my mother called *la tumba* (the tumb), inside which she kept piano scores and various objects. Obviously, a piano was a necessity: what girl of a good family could escape learning to play the piano? The fact that I evinced an interest and talent sharper than my sister's wouldn't have come to light without this piano which, with André's bust, dominated the living room. And in my father's bedroom, facing his bed, hung a portrait of Andreika on his deathbed, suffering, unconscious, his eyes closed, covered to the neck with a red quilt. An awful portrait, without talent or style, and in frightful taste.

How I hated this portrait! Whatever my young life was capable of doing, Andreika did it better. He was so sweet, so talented, so affectionate! Everything in him was oh so

128

admirable. I must have been about seven, when one day, pushed to the limit, I seized a bottle of ink and threw it with all my might at that horrible painting, splattering it with black. After that, neither my mother nor my father ever spoke to me about Andreika again — a heavy silence, which we all got used to. But by that time the harm had been profoundly embedded in my malleable psyche. Only many decades later was I able to find and root it out.

And during all these times, which I have so thoroughly erased from my consciousness that very little remains in my memory, there was also the pressure to live up to my father's greatness. Georgians never ceased repeating: "Your father is such a great man! Few people in the world measure up to him. You're still young; you don't realize how important he is to us all, to all the Georgians, to all lovers of democracy. You must make yourself worthy of him, must merit the heritage you received at birth."

Not surprising then that I made myself Canadian! In that country I had no famous father, no Georgians preaching nostalgia, no model brother held as an example, no strange name! It was a country where I could wear the prestigious mantle of the hardened trapper, the obstinate gold miner, the adventurer of the Great North surrounded by his faithful dogs, where other humans were but faraway shadows that couldn't touch me.

**Running Away**

It was around that time that I tried to run away. I must have been quite conscious at bottom of the imaginary dimension of my purported life as a trapper in the Great North, of the absolute physical impossibility of even attempting to reach it. Thus when life's pressures became for me intolerable, when I felt the compulsion to do something about it—oh, in such a childish way —yet to actually take action, I turned to the sea as my avenue of escape. Most probably Pierre Loti, Jules Verne, Jack London, *The Red Pirate* had a lot to do with that yearning. Certainly nothing in my family nor in my immediate circle linked or impelled me to the life of a sailor—yet today, at age 65, I have become an amateur sailor, and am writing these words during a brief stop on Cumberland Island, off the Atlantic coast of Florida, where I arrived on board the 130-foot schooner, *the Spirit of Massachusetts.*

I look back tenderly on that little boy who decided to run away from the paternal home, to flee school and his everyday circle, to forsake land and its swarming humanity in order to find freedom as a ship's boy aboard a sailing vessel from Brest, sailing capital of France. Obviously no other locality could satisfy this aspiration. Yes, I look back tenderly. He had only a vague idea of geography. All he knew was that he did not know how to travel directly from Paris to Brest, so that the simplest way was to follow the river Seine all the way to the ocean, then to turn left and continue along the shore: sooner or later he would get to Brest, he was convinced.

Although he had no idea of the distance thus many times multiplied, he well knew it would be impossible on foot. He needed a bicycle, the bicycle he coveted but which his parents had not deemed appropriate to buy him. It is really amazing how need creates initiative. I cannot resurrect the details of the enormous undertaking it must have been for a little boy of twelve to acquire a bicycle without stealing one—an idea that never crossed his mind. As for money, however, he well knew where to look: in his father's desk drawer, from where he had often seen him take some cash. But where would he find a bike and who would sell to a little boy a contraption worth some 85 francs, a considerable amount of money in those times?

I remember talking "business" with the owner of a bicycle shop near the metro station *La Motte-Piquet Grenelle*, quite a distance from my paternal Vanves. How did I get there, to this shop in *La Motte-Piquet Grenelle*? I have no recollection. I simply see myself several times in that shop with its enchanting aromas, saying I don't know what to the owner. I must certainly have been convincing, since one good morning when I should have been at school, I appeared in his shop holding a beautiful one-hundred franc banknote, in exchange for which he delivered into my hands a brand new bicycle — how my heart beat! — and almost 15 francs, my capital.

I well knew where the Seine was and reached it quickly. But once I was on its banks, a first difficulty confronted me: which way to go? Where was the sea? To the left? To the right? And I can still see that kid throwing bits of wood in the water, trying to determine the direction of the current, for he knew quite well that rivers run towards the ocean. But he wasn't counting on the eddies, the countercurrents. His wood chips refused to yield a clear indication. Finally he made up his mind and set out on his bicycle, but I don't know if it was in the right direction.

As it turned out, it didn't matter. The streets did not follow the river. Suddenly they would veer to the right, or to the left; and in order not to get lost, he figured, he would go down on the banks, bicycle in hand, where it took him forever to make his way through piles of stone, mountains of gravel, heaps of sand, all sorts of obstacles blocking his path.

Sometimes the banks would end abruptly in a dead-end, and he would have to backtrack, find a ramp leading to the quay above, and start all over again. Once more he found himself on a bank down below the street level, enormous piles of sand, stones, cement surrounding him on every side ... and night came, with its terrors. I see him fighting his way back up to the street, assaulted by phantasms. I see him glimpsing far away a yellowish light, approaching it, hesitating, finally pushing the cafe door it was shining from. I see him surrounded by grownups questioning him, I see him with a policeman, and then he finds himself back home, a terrifying emptiness in his body and soul, emptiness from which he must push away, oh how horrible, the black cloud of shame: shame of having abandoned the undertaking at the first obstacle, and shame that was poured on him for having undertaken it at all.

## First Love

We are lying on a bed, side by side. We don't even touch. Simply to be thus, so close, without talking, without moving, without thinking, gives me a warm feeling of well-being without the slightest hint of illicit aspirations.

I am perhaps 12 years old. She is the same age, or near enough. I can still see her, a bit dumpy, straight auburn hair framing her face, splotched complexion, dressed with a long-sleeved blouse and a skirt reaching to mid-calf, of a brownish color. It was the era when the rule was for children to take a siesta after lunch, at least during vacations. And thus automatically, without even thinking about it, as if it were our right, we dutifully obey, together of course, as we had been together all day ever since she arrived in the boarding-house my mother organized every summer in order to be able to take us out of Paris for the long vacations.

I don't remember her name. That's not surprising, you would say, since it was almost three quarters of a century ago! But when that episode would occasionally come back to me throughout the years, not a single time could I remember it – which tends to show that her identity didn't matter much, even though she was everything for me in that eternal slice of time, that was nevertheless oh so short. She thus remains without a name, without characteristics, with nothing surrounding her. SHE in capital letters, as the 19th century romantics would have baptized her. A SHE in a pure state, since she was a SHE that I had internalized, representing all my aspirations, all that I was missing, all that I needed in order to complete myself.

We are thus lying on that bed, side by side, the door of the room wide open, this July afternoon, in the country house close to the Yonne river that my mother had rented for the summer. Victor happens by in the corridor, sees us, steps into the room. He is a grown-up, in my eyes he is a man, although he must have been no more than eighteen. He comes closer, looks at us, and says: "Don't do anything stupid". He lingers a bit. We don't move. After a few moments he goes away. I remain lying there, not moving, in total incomprehension: "Anything stupid? What can he mean?" And I forget him immediately. I feel so good just like that, alongside her. Time slows, the siesta lasts, and lasts …

It must be a few days later. We are in the woods, she and I, not too far from the house, sitting on a rock, holding each-other tightly, face against face, body against body. My left arm is around her, my right hand is nestled on her naked thigh against her buttock, a place oh so warm, so delicious. I can still see her coarse white cotton panties, but how come I see them, since we are embracing so closely, cheek to cheek?

We do not kiss. I do not think we ever kissed, not on the mouth, not even on the cheek or anywhere else. As for me, and perhaps she also, I feel nothing of what I later would learn to be sexual desire. Really nothing, nothing at all, no physiological, nor even mental manifestation.

We remain thus, in each other's arms, without thinking, without moving. Once again time does not exist. I vaguely realize that daylight is fading, that night is getting closer, but just like that, in an abstract fashion that does not apply to me, to us. It is the height of summer, daylight lasts until ten. We have missed dinner, they must wonder where we have disappeared. After all we are only 12 years old! But that thought would come to me only much later. At the moment I just *am*, we just *are*. And since we *are* we need nothing, we have no desire, no wish to change position, move, explore by touch any part of the other's body. We *are*, in the twilight.

And then Victor appears, softly walking on the path cushioned with pine needles. He stops in front of us – we don't move – and simply says: "Oh! Here you are! Well, time to go home."

*Growing up in Leuville*

We unglue ourselves, we separate. With Victor we come back to the house, one or two kilometers away. No one says anything, nobody scolds us, reproaches us for anything, even though for two hours everybody was searching for us, fearing a drowning in the nearby Yonne river or another accident. Simply they separate us without fuss, I in my room, she in hers.

The following day she had disappeared. I imagine her parents took her away. I never saw her again. The most surprising, when revisiting this episode, is that I never missed her, that I never regretted her, at least consciously. But I keep forever the memory of our short magnetic embraces, and above all I can still feel that hand on her naked thigh, not moving, not seeking, just resting there, in total bliss ...

**Playing Hooky**

Hidden behind a flowerbed, I wait impatiently for the church bell to strike 4 p.m. Only then can I show myself and go back home. It is now three weeks that I have been playing truant, and I am fed up! I think with envy about my classmates who sensibly follow the fixed ruts of their schoolboys' life: at school from eight thirty to noon, then from one to four, when most of them go back home. And me? Like them, I leave home shortly after eight. Like them, I walk towards the entrance of the Lycée Michelet, two blocks away. But not like them at all, I quickly run to the park down by the church, where I am reduced to hiding from everyone's eyes behind bushes and trees: playing hooky isn't fun! I have to hide because I am just about 13 years old, and any adult seeing me strolling about during school hours feels entitled to question me: "What are you doing here? Why aren't you in school? Your parents know where you're going? What's your name? Where do you live?"

Even though I can think on my feet and manage to come up with satisfactory answers, I know it's only a question of time. I'll end up getting mixed up, contradict myself, and thus

134

be brought to the school authorities and to my parents, with horrifying consequences I do not dare imagine! But it's been going on for three long weeks, and I am up to here. I am afraid of being found out. I hope to be found out. How to escape the condition I managed to entangle myself in, not without difficulties?

I had to display quite a bit of ingenuity to escape the tight net of controls that govern a schoolboy's life. A single unauthorized absence, and immediately a letter is sent to the parents, which in those times would get to its destination the following morning. If no answer, a phone call ensues, followed by other letters or communications from the school authorities.

But I knew how to foil them all. The postman would come by around eight in the morning. I would manage to be in front of the door, as if by chance, and would intercept any communication coming from the Lycée. In addition, I had discovered that the telephone line had a fuse, just like the electric lines. Before leaving, I pulled out the fuse, certain as I was that, given my parents total ignorance of things mechanical, they wouldn't even notice that the telephone was cut on purpose, and would attribute any malfunction to some vagary of those modern instruments, in which one shouldn't have too much confidence. When I came back at noon, I would put back the fuse, secure in my knowledge that no one in the school administration would telephone during the sacred hour of lunch. Then, going out again, I'd once more take out the fuse, putting it back around 4.30 p.m., when I knew the Lycée offices would be closed.

In those times, the telephone was still a luxury. People used it sparingly, preferring to write or to go in person. Thus my sabotage would go unnoticed during the few days it was necessary. Besides I had made sure that, when the fuse was removed, the line would ring with a busy signal, as if the phone was in use.

Third line of defense: As any schoolboy worthy of his name, I had learned to forge my father's signature, which was quite distinctive, by placing one of his letters against a window pane and tracing it on a piece of paper. Since my legitimate letters of excuse were usually written by myself in my own handwriting and signed by him, the authorities were always taken in. So many excuses I had thus bestowed on myself, not only for unauthorized absences or unready homework, but also to escape punishment.

Teachers had several means of exacting discipline. First came extra homework of the type: "Write 100 times the sentence: "I will not play tic tack toe in the classroom." I remember spending many hours putting together a five-pronged pen, with which to write five sentences at the same time! That it took me a lot longer to do it that way didn't faze me in the slightest, since that was inventiveness, and the normal way would be unmitigated boredom. (In a somewhat similar way, I used to prepare for cheating at exams by condensing and writing answers on tiny pieces of paper or on my body ... with the result that I hardly ever needed to consult these notes, since this time-consuming process imprinted the answers in my brain!)

Teachers could also make us stay in school after hours. If one wouldn't stay, the punishment was doubled. If the offense warranted it, the student was forced to spend a day or a half-day in school on Sunday or Thursday, since there were no classes those days – (we did go to school Saturdays, though). But I had discovered that if once again I wouldn't comply and present myself in school for the punishment, the next step would be expulsion for one, two, or more days! That is to say, instead of being chained in prison for additional days, one could gain freedom—always making sure that my parents would somehow not know anything about the state of affairs. I wasn't slow to take advantage of such a boon, forging letters of excuse left and right. In the end it is true that these scattered days of freedom, stolen here and there from life, acquired a most exceptional taste.

But what's good once in a while becomes heavy if it lasts. This time it went on, and on, and on! I don't recall how I had managed to tie myself in knots, to the point that I was totally paralyzed behind my flowerbed, without the slightest inkling of how to escape from that situation. Finally, of course, I was found out. I still remember the enormous relief I felt, while I was being berated and tried to look penitent. I believe this is when I first discovered the price of freedom and understood somewhat why so many people remain in their way of life, even if disagreeable, rather than risk uncertainty ... not that this ever applied to me in a serious way.

As a result of that last feat, at the end of the school year, I was expelled from the Lycée Michelet. When classes resumed in the fall, I went to the Lycée Buffon, much farther from home—a school which agreed to accept me.

**The House in Vanves**

My poor parents! I feel sure that the closeness of the Lycée Michelet had been one of the main reasons they had decided to settle on that ordinary street in Vanves, on the outskirts of Paris, in a modest row house with a small garden in the back, for which I feel not the slightest nostalgia. When I first had to go to school, at age six, they registered me at the Lycée Michelet in the 12th class (equivalent to the American 1st grade), but the very first day I managed to get lost. The experience was so traumatic for me that they had to take me out and send me to the town's elementary school, which was much farther away. And now, after less than three years at the Lycée, I managed to be expelled! My parents could just as well have chosen to settle anywhere else, in more practical quarters. But they got used to this place: the house fit their needs, and thus they remained there until their deaths, my father's in 1953, and my mother's in 1968.

Many years later in 1992, I had the curiosity to drive through the Rue Solférino in Vanves with my sister, to have a look at the house where my parents lived for so long. It was still there but with a sign announcing: For Sale. We were thus able to go inside.   The house had been repaired, repainted, rearranged. There were now two bathrooms. A long balcony had been added above the small garden lying fallow, where the old plum trees still rose to the sky. Contrary to what usually happens when one revisits places of one's childhood, it seemed to me lighter and bigger than the shrunken house of my remembrances, even though I know it couldn't have changed its size, squeezed as it was between two adjoining villas. In the basement, from which the celebrated coal furnace had been expelled a long time ago, we found my father's bed boards. The owner of the house, Monsieur Régnier, who lived there after my mother's death, had carefully preserved them as possible memorabilia. Monsieur Régnier was also discussing the possibility of asking town hall for permission to affix to the facade a plate commemorating the long years my parents lived there. But he too passed away before those projects could be realized.

My sister Nathela liked the house very much; she would readily have lived there again, if she had been able to afford it. As for me, it left me cold. Nothing would induce me to live there, perhaps because for me the remembrances attached to it carry mostly negative associations. Yet many warm feelings are also present in my soul, first among them those attached to Anush and Mishush, our family cats.

**My Mother was a Cat**

Anush was a Persian Blue. I cannot picture her in my mind as the kitten she must have been when she first appeared in my young life. For me she will always be the Mother Cat, affectionate but stern. Not only was she a mother to her own offsprings, whom she fabricated twice a year regular as clockwork, but she was also a mother to me, to the family dog, and even to a sick chicken that my mother installed under the kitchen sink in an attempt to save its life.

Anush adopted it immediately, and I carry inside me the image of this tiny yellow chick tucked between the enormous front paws of that monster cat who licked it tenderly while it kept sneezing because the whiskers tickled its nose. I do not remember what happened to the chicken; for all I know, it died of old age, since my mother tended to keep her pet poultry and rabbits forever.

Soon another addition to our household appeared: Minush, who, for some reason, was the only one of Anush's offspring to remain with us. Minush was also a Persian Blue, — by some vagary of genes, since Anush was by no means choosy about her suitors. But while Anush remained always slender and quick-moving, Minush was plump, slow, and easy-going; and while Anush's expression was always firm, stern, and decisive, Minush's remained at all times vague and somewhat nonplussed. Of course Anush lorded it over Minush, never allowing her to forget the respect and obedience that parents were then used to expect from their children.

Twice a year, for as long as I can remember, Anush and Minush would disappear for days at a time in response to the ancient call of nature. Anush would reappear first, prim and proper, as if nothing had happened. Minush would come back days later, unashamed of the state she was in: sloppy, dirty, mangy, her fur matted here and there by some unspeakable goo, — no doubt, given the smell, the result of some male cat's possessive spraying. Usually she would be given a bath. A bath! To a cat! But then, Minush was in such a state of bliss and exhaustion that she didn't seem to mind. The bath was of course necessary before allowing her in the house. One whiff of her interesting fragrance would have been enough to chase even a skunk away!

With free access to the big wide world yonder, both Anush and Minush would become pregnant and give birth at practically the same time. In those days it was the custom to get rid of all but one kitten out of each litter (I never wondered how), since to eliminate them entirely would be cruel to the mother, and who could afford to take care of them all? (A brief calculation shows that if each litter consists of an average of four kittens, half of which are female, a single mother cat would beget 1458 offsprings in three years! )

This system worked quite well with Minush, who could not count. But Anush knew quite well when she didn't have her right number of babies. Not being given to complaints, she'd take action: she would find Minush's nest, grab the lone kitten that was there, and bring it to her own secret abode. Even if she could not count, though, poor Minush well knew the difference between the positive and the negative, between one or more kittens and no kitten at all. But she could never figure out what had happened, and there she was forlornly wandering throughout the house wailing her sorrows. In self-defense, everybody would embark on a hunt to find Anush's hiding place, grab that extra kitten, and return it to Minush so she would shut up. Of course, as soon as Minush had to leave her baby even for a few moments, there was Anush kidnapping it anew, and the whole rigmarole had to be gone through again.

Not only would Anush rule Minush and whichever kittens happened to be living with us, but she would ·also terrorize the neighborhood dogs, and of course the family pooch, Lady.

Lady was black, nondescript, temperamental, and given to snip at people from behind. She had a perennial skin affliction which was usually treated with some foul-smelling substance, and, despite many attempts, refused to have anything to do with any male dog, so that she remained a virgin all her life.

In theory Lady lived in a sort of doghouse under the porch's stone steps. In practice she lived in the basement where, in winter, she would find a comfortable nook right next to the furnace. Lady had thus no particular attachment to her private apartments under the porch, except twice a year: that was when Anush decided to take them over as a perfect place to raise her offsprings.

Lady would then feel being taken advantage of, and would bother the whole neighborhood with her moans and whimpers, not daring to come anywhere near her doghouse, from the entrance of which Anush would be calmly watching her antics.

This would go on for some weeks. Then, the kittens old enough to go out and play, Anush would abandon the doghouse, in which Lady would immediately lose all interest. By then, though, she had learned her lesson anew, and would never dare harm the kittens, who used to play with her tail or clamber all over her, Anush, never entirely trustful, vigilantly sitting by her head as if to say :"Behave yourself, or else!"

I have only faint recollections of being caressed or kissed by my mother, nor do I remember any particular feelings of tenderness and confidence towards her. Not that she did not love me, perhaps even too much in her own way, but she was always busy with politics as well as with the chores of everyday living. She was in fact quite a remarkable woman whom I learned to accept and respect later in life. Is that why I used to feel closer to animals and children than to adults, even when I became one myself?

In any case it is upon Anush and Minush that I bestowed my affections and from whom I received the warmth and emotional support that I didn't get from the family circle. How many times have I not buried my face in the moist and fragrant fur of Anush's belly? How many times did I not confide in her, protected by her purring presence, the childish sorrows that descended upon me, which I only now begin to realize influenced me so much in my whole life?

To wake up in the morning surrounded by the warm presence of my two mother-cats was to color the day with diaphanous light. Minush used to crawl under the sheet and settle alongside my legs, occasionally kicking a fuss because she would forget how to crawl out again... while Anush, more independent-minded, would settle on the pillow right against my head, which would reverberate with her approving purrs.

One of the happiest memories of my childhood comes back fresh to my mind. I open my eyes, wide awake. Moonlight is streaking into my bedroom through the half open French window. On the night-table next to me is Anush, straight and intent. Minush is in her usual sloppy sitting posture at the foot of the bed. Rhythmic dull sounds break the stillness: it is Lady's tail thumping on the carpet. Several kittens are madly playing throughout the room. (Why more than two? I don't know.) They bounce from bed to table and from rug to chair, they run across my body, they sneak through Lady's legs. Well trained by Anush, Lady doesn't dare take part in the game, but follows it with great attention. It is a living painting, suspended in an eternal instant.

I think I am remaining awake, but I must have fallen asleep since all of a sudden the scene has changed without my being aware that time has elapsed. The moon rays reach the room in a much sharper slant. An instant before they traced an oblong on the floor, now they stretch thinly across table and chair. There is a black stain on the rug: Lady, sleeping all curled-up.

The kittens also are sleeping, bunched together in the hollow of my knees. Minush is still at the foot of the bed, but Anush has disappeared. I just know she's at work, patiently waiting in front of a mouse hole somewhere, a posture she's quite able to sustain for a whole day and night without twitching a whisker. The room is now completely silent. I feel surrounded by the living warmth of my tribal friends. Calm, drowsiness, fading moon-rays... In the morning I go to school, all alone.

I don't remember exactly when and how our long association came to an end. I was over 20 years old, probably closer to 23. My parents were still living in the same house with Anush and Minush. Lady had disappeared long before, hit by a bus, I was told. As befitted my young manhood I used to wander the world, living here and there, but always coming back for a day or two at a time.

When I was back the old relationship with my mother-cats resumed as if no time had passed, including playing the piano with Minush on my lap and Anush perched on top. Eventually my returns became less and less frequent. During that period, somehow, somewhere, Anush and Minush departed the house and life, discreetly, all by themselves, as proper cats are wont to do.

My mother lived on many years, active and involved, until the ripe age of 90. To this day, though, if I think of a child's need for love and affection, it is Anush and Minush who spring to mind, forever alive in my inner eternity.

## How to Become Stateless by Trying Very Hard

In 1942, in the middle of the war in occupied Paris, I decided to renounce my French citizenship and to take the Georgian nationality: all by myself, just like that, nobody prodding me; when it was already obvious that the Germans wouldn't succeed in dismantling the USSR, when it was already certain that Georgia would not be liberated, and even though I hardly spoke a word of Georgian, much less could read or write the language.

When I was a child my parents usually spoke Russian to each other, as my mother, who was Russian, did not know Georgian. Since both were fluent in French, that is the language I grew up with, at home and at school. When I was in my early teens, my father started speaking to me in Georgian, my mother in Russian, but by then I had fallen into the habit of answering in French.

I had a passion for traditional Georgian folk music, which is indeed worthy of such a love, with its incredibly daring polyphonies, rhythms, and counterpoints. Indeed musicologists the world over consider the Georgian popular music to be one of the highlights of folkloric art.

In the 1970's, when the Americans sent up the first spatial vehicle to escape solar attraction and continue toward galactic spaces, it was decided to put aboard a very limited load of documents, objects, recordings, and films describing the human race. This was done in the most unlikely but not impossible case that this rocket might one faraway day be intercepted by an unimaginable civilization ...at least in one million years at the very earliest. Among the few musical recordings rocketed into the unimaginable was a Georgian Gurian song, selected by the musicologist Alan Lomax, as one of the best examples of human musical creativity.

An amusing side-light: Not knowing the Georgian language, the American authorities had the words of the song translated into English just to make sure they didn't express anything positive about Communism or Stalin. How silly can one be!

Despite my fascination with the Georgian folkloric songs, it never occurred to me to learn the words, even though they are an integral part of its riches. I admired it strictly from a musical standpoint, without attempting to analyze or transcribe it, but rather by adapting its themes in some personal compositions.

I didn't realize that in so doing I was temporarily locking my musical gifts into a narrow cage, from which I was unable to extricate the principles which would have allowed me to develop. For me that cage proved a dead end for many years, since I remained totally separated from the vigorous evolution of this folklore within its own society in Georgia proper.

Was it because of this musical influence that I found myself pushed into that other dead end: Choosing the status of "Refugee of Georgian Origin" i.e., statelessness, over French citizenship? Or was it a confluence of circumstances pushing me into that dead-end direction? It is clear that the propaganda with which the Georgian community assailed me constantly had a great deal to do with it, as did the unformulated desire to make my father happy, since he was the incarnation of the Georgian spirit.

In addition I had become alienated from everything, even myself: purposeless, powerless, lacking ambition, lacking definite rules. I felt trapped in this wartime Paris, on top of feeling trapped for quite a while by Georgia, ever since my childish attempts to escape only resulted in total alienation. Hopelessly caught between my hate of Nazism and the simultaneous desire for a German victory that would liberate Georgia, I saw the door to possible eventual Georgian citizenship as the only viable one that remained open to me, a door which I believed could lead... where? I had no idea, but the fact that I perceived there an opening was all that counted.

The actual event turned out to be rather comical. I must first say that it was not easy. I was legally French. I therefore had to repudiate my French citizenship —what a strong word! — — and adopt Georgian citizenship. But to do so, I had to prove who I was, and to accomplish this I needed to prove that my parents were indeed my parents.

Another obstacle: French law stated that this procedure was allowed only during the year following the age of majority, which was then 21. But in times of war majority was lowered to 18, the law, in its wisdom, thus allowing the very young to enlist without parental consent. I was already in my 21st year, it was a time of war; therefore, it was three years too late to make the change.

It was interesting to see the French authorities approach the problem simply as a bureaucratic problem, without ever considering what it meant. Nobody, no one discussed with me if this procedure made any sense, if it would be beneficial to me. Thus the problem was considered strictly in the abstract: how to follow the letter of the law in order to obtain the desired result. I don't know how the bureaucrats solved the question of the three-year delay, but solve it they did. I still remember the triumphant look of the official who announced the news to me as if it were a ray of light in his gray daily routine.

The problem with my parents was that neither of them had a birth certificate, and they didn't possess a marriage license either.

French law provided that in such cases the declaration of three witnesses older than the concerned parties could replace the official documents. But where to find these three witnesses? There was only one Georgian older than my father's 76 years, our archeologist Ephtimé Takaishvili, but that was all. Finally the bureaucrats accepted the principle of two other witnesses about the same age as my father, and then had to settle for just one Georgian, since there was no one else. They gave as a reason for this unaccustomed leniency, that because of my father's age, it would be impossible to find anyone older. Remember that in those times a man of 60 was considered a doddering oldster, and few people reached 70. Thus my father at age 76 and in full possession of his faculties was a rarity.

Finally the required papers for my change of citizenship were collected. I can still see my father and his associates briskly walking through the streets of Vanves to sign them, Ephtimé limping behind them. In a dark office, on a gloomy winter day, I too signed the documents stating that I was giving up my French citizenship. For a moment at least it seemed that I had accomplished a great thing. My father was very proud... and then it was forgotten by all, except the French authorities. And that's how I became stateless.

Would I have pushed this endeavor to completion if I had thought it through, if I had known, really known, that by abandoning of my own free will the French nationality, which was mine by right, I would bring upon myself so many annoyances, complications, bureaucratic difficulties and obstacles of all kinds?

Becoming stateless meant that I received from police headquarters a foreign resident I.D. (similar to the American green card); that I had to stand in line at least once a year in a police precinct to renew the residence permit; that I would be interrogated about my activities by one of the two bureaucrats assigned to the job: one skinny, sickly complexion, glasses, jittery, and the other stocky, reddish complexion, badly dressed: we all referred to them as the "thin" and the "fat". And they knew so much, about everybody! Where did they get all this information? Who was close enough to me to be able to inform them in such detail?

I remember that one day the fat one told me: "We know that you are still a student, that you often spend time in the Dupont café, that usually you are alone, that you don't mix with the groups of punks that gather there. An advice: continue to avoid them, if not it could end up badly for you!"

[All governments are alike. In the 80's, after I had been living in the U.S. over 20 years and became an American citizen, out of curiosity I requested my file, if any, as allowed under the Freedom of Information Act. After a long delay I indeed received it: some 12 pages, out of which at least nine were almost completely blacked out except for a few meaningless words.

[The other pages, partially blackened, had wrong factual information about my residences, plus detailed accurate facts such as which coffee shops I used to frequent in Greenwich Village. Here again, who was close enough to me to know such details and was in a position to snitch to the authorities, and why?]

Yes, to be stateless meant to be subjected to all kinds of bureaucratic complications, being unable to travel freely, to be compelled to justify one's existence, to have to obtain permits for what a French national could get or do as a matter of course.

And it is for this that I gave up the French nationality to become officially *Refugee of Georgian Origin.*

**Fast Forward 50 Years**

More than a half century later, on 26 May 1998, date of the 80th anniversary of the Georgian Declaration of Independence – an historical event that was promulgated by my father from the Hall of Mirrors of the former Vice-Roy palace in Tbilisi – Eduard Shevardnadze, President of the newly independent Georgia, bestowed upon me the dignity of Honorary Citizen.

And then, in 2004, the next President of Georgia Michael Saakashvili personally presented my sister Nathela and me

with official papers making us full-fledged citizens.

After the ceremony a reporter asked her: "How does it feel to be Georgian?"

To which she replied: "I have always been Georgian. The only difference is that now I have the papers to prove it."

# Part Two:

# Tbilisi, at Long Last

# 10. NEW YORK – TBILISI

**The Occasion**

At long last in September 1990 the long-awaited occasion to go to Georgia for the very first time of my long life came to pass. Already my daughter Nicole had spent time in Tbilisi as a student, but for me it had proven to be hitherto impossible: a country's memory is very long and bureaucratic memory even more so: half a century is nothing! Thus, as the son of Noé Jordania, a social-democrat president of independent Georgia at the end of World War One, it had been unthinkable to obtain a visa for the Soviet Union, even after the death of Stalin, who considered my father as one of his greatest personal enemies. But with *Glasnost* and *Perestroika*, with the fall of the Berlin Wall just a few months before in November 1989, things got better, the Soviet paranoia abated, and a voyage to the Soviet Union became possible even for those who had been excluded.

The pretext was offered by my niece Ethery Pagava, the well-known Paris ballet dancer and choreographer, and her husband Jacques Douai, a folk singer famous in all French-speaking countries. At the time I lived in New York City, thus I knew nothing of their projects when I received a phone call from Jacques:

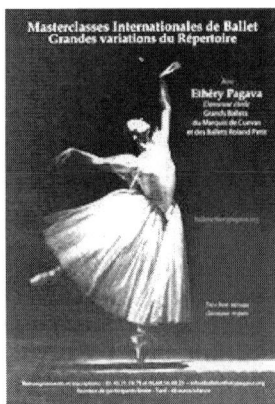

"You remember how we enjoyed making music together, you at the piano and me at the guitar and singing? It went very well, with no rehearsal, just improvising and fooling around. Well, how would you like to do it again, this time on tour?" And he explained that Ethery and he had organized a tour in Moscow, Georgia and Armenia to present a combination of dance by the Ballets Ethery Pagava and his singing act.

My first reaction was of course surprise: nothing had prepared me for this. Then surprise gave way to an objection on artistic grounds, strangely enough: "It has been a really long time since I played the piano in public, professionally. I am not sure I would be up to the challenge."

"Yes, I understand how you feel, but accompanying my songs is really very easy, technically speaking," Jacques insisted.

"What about your usual pianist?"

"Well, he cannot free himself for so long, and also, frankly, it would cost me much too much to pay him for all his time for several weeks, instead of compensating him one gig at a time, as usual."

"But what about visas? Permissions? I may well be blacklisted in the Soviet Union. And what about the KGB? Remember what happened here in New York a few years ago? Maybe they are still after us; it might not be advisable to travel there yet. What do you think?"

I was referring to events that occurred in a couple of years previously when Ethery and Jacques stopped by in New York at the end of their tour of French-speaking Canada.

## A Dinner with the KGB

I have always been fond of those types of adventure stories that begin in a low key with just a small twist in the fabric of everyday life, as exemplified by Eric Ambler and other old-fashioned masters of the genre. So it is in a way surprising that I did not recognize immediately as suspicious the events through which the KGB and, for all I know, the CIA and other intelligence agencies obtained close-up photographs of myself and members of my family, as well as a field-agent assessment of our activities or lack thereof in the political sphere.

This lack of recognition on my part may well have come from the fact that it never occurred to me that the Soviets would have any interest in me whatsoever — and if they did, why go about getting information in such a roundabout, obvious and clumsy way? Yes, my father had been the very first democratic president of Georgia and a leader of the Mensheviks, those fellow revolutionaries and arch-enemies of the Bolsheviks that Lenin and Stalin hated and despised even more than they ever did Western Capitalists. But that was many years before.

As for myself, I had never indulged in those politics that constituted the life blood of my father and his associates in exile. I was born in France, where my parents settled after the Red Amy overran the Georgian republic back in 1921. I grew up in that double cultural environment peculiar to political émigrés families, going to a French school, participating in everyday French life, yet never deeply being part of that society, while practically all my childhood friends and acquaintances were children of émigrés like myself. Yet for me the Old Country remained something totally remote, and my interest when I grew older remained of an intellectual rather than emotional nature.

Thus in New York city where I had been living for the last 20 years, I rarely saw my compatriots of the Georgian Colony — a small group of mainly elderly gentlemen and ladies given to meet periodically and reminisce about the heroic times when the yoke of the Tsarist imperial power was shaken off, the foundation of a democratic state established, the dream of independence nurtured, only to be shattered seemingly forever after a scant three years of freedom. Never mind that some of our elderly Georgians were no more than 8 or 10 years old in those heroic times: legend and reality were confounded, and they all believed deeply in their own great deeds and awareness of the everyday presence of their lost motherland.

The events I am about to relate occurred in May 1987 in New York, at the occasion of the annual Georgian dinner commemorating the Georgian declaration of independence — an occasion for national food, songs, and maudlin speeches meandering through the lapses of aging minds.

That year, the date of the dinner coincided with my niece Ethery Pagava's visit to New York. Ethery, a well-known ballet dancer and choreographer, was traveling with her husband, Jacques Douai, a popular French folk singer, who was just finishing a touring engagement in Canada and the U.S. Weeks before they had accepted an invitation to attend this dinner celebration, their participation promising to add luster to what had become an ingrown event attended year after year by a dwindling audience of the same participants.

A few days before the dinner, I received a phone call from Paul Gargomadze, the President of the Georgian Association in the US, a nice, fatherly man in his late sixties, who had retired from his garage business and dedicated his dwindling energies to the Cause. He first inquired about my niece's arrival, to check that all was going well – they were arriving from Montreal the very afternoon of the dinner. He then proceeded to explain that he wanted very much for all of us to meet a certain couple, he American, she a Soviet citizen of Georgian descent, who had sought him out and wanted to get acquainted with members of the Georgian colony.

Paul explained that the man, Bert, was a book executive working for an American scientific books publishing company, and that he specialized in selling and acquiring textbooks behind the Iron Curtain; that he very often traveled to the Soviet Union, and that he had met Svetlana, his soviet wife, at the Moscow State office of International Copyright where she worked as a translator.

156

He added that his wife, Svetlana, was of Georgian descent, spoke very well English, French, and other languages, but did not speak Georgian, despite the fact that both her parents were Georgians living in Moscow; that they were married not long ago, and that she retained her soviet citizenship and passport, while he, of course, was American; and that they had bought a house in Glen Gove, Long Island, where they had settled recently.

When I asked Paul how he had met them, he explained they contacted him in his capacity as President of the Georgian Association. Their reason was that Svetlana — a Russian name, by the way —, being of Georgian descent, wanted to meet and become friends with other Georgians in her new country. He said he would like all of us to come to his home in Queens for lunch, and later we would all go to the annual dinner which was to be held in the Estonian House on East 34th street in Manhattan.

I explained it would probably not be possible, as Ethery and Jacques were scheduled to land in Kennedy at 3 p.m., and by the time they would be at their hote, it would already be 5 pm at the earliest, assuming the plane was on time. Paul then said he would come pick us all up at the hotel to drive us to the dinner celebration. When I remonstrated that it would be just as easy for us to jump in a taxi, since the hotel was not far from 34th street, he insisted: "No, no, Ethery and Jacques are the guests of honor; the least I can do is to pick you all up myself." So it was agreed.

At the time of these events Ethery had retired from dancing, and was dedicating herself to choreography and teaching. She had been a star dancer in world-renowned ballet companies, and was the only one of our family to have ever set foot in the Soviet Union: in 1965 she was invited to Soviet Georgia to dance *Giselle* in the

157

state opera in Tbilisi — a departure from the usually prudent norms that the soviet authorities lived to regret: the news that the granddaughter of Noé Jordania, the one and only President of the Georgian Independent Republic, was to perform in Tbilisi brought huge crowds, as if more than 50 years had been erased, as if everyone remembered keenly my father's time and its dream of chaotic freedom. And when, at the official dinner honoring her as a dancer, she was asked to say a few words, she concluded her speech with a *Gaumarjos Damoukidebeli Sakartvelos* (Hail to independent Georgia) — to the glee of all and the consternation of party officials. The following day she was unceremoniously bundled off to the airport, all further shows cancelled, and, needless to say, she was never invited again.

That Saturday, my niece and her husband arrived late, their plane having been delayed, — a common occurrence, — so that it was already 7 pm when Peggy and I joined them at their hotel on Lexington and 59th street. They had barely time to get settled and refreshed when Paul came to pick us up, as he had insisted doing. Thus we went on our merry way, as we thought, to join the Georgian celebration.

I vaguely noticed that Paul was driving down Second Avenue, which was a way to go to the Estonian house on 34th street where the dinner was to take place. All of a sudden Peggy exclaimed: "Redjeb, look where we are! Where are we going?" I looked up, and sure enough we were on the approach ramp to the Queen's midtown tunnel!

"Paul, what's going on?" I exclaimed. "Aren't we going to the Estonian house? Did you miss your turn, or something?"

Paul replied, seemingly unruffled: "I thought we would first go to my house in Queens to meet the people I told you about, Bert and Svetlana, and later we'll join the Georgians."

"But Paul," I exclaimed again, "It will be much too late to go! Indeed I don't understand!" And Jacques chimed in, in French, since his English was poor: "Mais c'est un vrai kidnapping!" *(It's a real kidnapping!)*

"Don't worry, all will be just fine", Paul reassured us, while Ethery, in her calm little voice proposed " You should turn right back, we promised to join the celebration of our independence day, not go somewhere else for I don't know what!"

Well, despite our remonstrations, nothing doing, Paul was determined, so that finally we resigned ourselves and went to his house, where his wife the Baroness and a sumptuous dinner awaited us, and of course the Soviet-American couple.

"Are you a dues-paying member of the Georgian Association?" Bert kept asking insistently, time and time again. He was a stout fellow, ruddy faced, crude features, horn-rimmed glasses, graying hair combed sideways with a parting line, with the hearty artificial manner of the salesman. "Dues paying" seemed to be for him very important. Throughout the evening, he kept harping on that theme — Oh shades of Senator McCarthy's *"dues paying members of the communist party"*.

His wife Svetlana was tall, slim, blonde, very pretty, with quite a subdued manner in total contrast with her husband's gruff heartiness. Her English was indeed very good, even when using those idiomatic expressions that come and go in the vernacular. It was hardly believable she had been living in the States a scant three months. She explained she learned English in Moscow, that she had been long employed in the copyright department of the State Scientific Publishers Board, and that she had had previous occasion to travel to the US, albeit for short visits only.

In personality and manners, in fact, she presented such a contrast with Bert that it created a strong feeling of plain wrongness to think of them as husband and wife — although god knows there are so many unlikely pairs around. That feeling of wrongness was reinforced by the fact that throughout the evening, whenever one of us would start talking with her, even if Bert was engaged in conversation at the other end of the living room, he would somehow instantly appear at her elbow and take over the conversation — in all the world as if he were afraid she might say something wrong, or even establish a slight personal contact out of his control. For instance, when Peggy kindly offered to show Svetlana around the city, and they already had made arrangements to meet, Bert intervened out of nowhere: "No, that won't be possible, my wife is much too busy these days."

But the main, salient point is that throughout the evening she was snapping photos of everybody, most insistently of me and my niece. She had several of those small disposable cameras with built-in flash, would come right close, and with a nice smile as if apologetic for being so engrossed with her new toy, would snap the shutter. "For my parents", she would say, explaining they would be so pleased to see recent photos of my father the President's family. Face, profile right, profile left, close up, whole bust, full size... she must have taken a good dozen photos of each of us.

And meantime, Bert kept harping on my being or not being a dues-paying member of the Georgian Association, and kept offering to bring clandestinely into the Soviet Union anything we might want to send to anyone.

"We go there very often, and no one questions us or searches our luggage, so that you can entrust to us anything you'd rather not have the Soviet authorities see," he kept offering, repeatedly. The whole thing was so blatant that Jacques, in French, and some of us in English asked, half in jest: "Which of you is CIA, and which KGB?" Of course they never acknowledged the question, let alone answered.

The evening finally drew to a close. We never got to join the other Georgians at the gathering we were supposed to attend — although we did talk on the phone to some of our friends there. Then, Paul drove us back to Manhattan, totally puzzled by the events of the evening.

One thing seemed obvious: within a few days, those photos and a detailed report would be in the hands of the KGB and, perhaps, the CIA ... and that seemed to be the whole purpose of that evening. But why go to such convoluted extremities to obtain these photos? As my niece said: "We are all hams at heart, if they wanted photos, we would have been just delighted to pose for them at the dinner."

So why did Paul change at the last moment the long-held plans to go to that Georgian dinner party? Why, instead, take us to his house for the whole evening, to meet privately with Bert and Svetlana? Why offend the other Georgians, when this Soviet-American couple could just as well come to the party and take our photo there?

No ready answer came to mind. Neither I nor my niece were ever active in politics. The times of my father's importance have been over more than 60 years. We, his family, could not possibly be of any interest to the so-called Georgian in Moscow that Svetlana claimed her father to be, nor could we represent any threat to the Soviet Government, by the remotest flight of imagination. Or ... could we, somehow?

The other question was: what kind of hold these two characters had on Paul, that they could make him practically kidnap us and bring us to them, in his own home, on the very day of the annual dinner of our association, of which by right he should have been the main host and speaker, and where Ethery and Jacques were supposed to be the guests of honor? Did they know of something shady in his past? Or did they threaten to do something bad to members of his family back in the Soviet Union? In any case it must have been something powerful for him to go against all the rule of hospitality and simple politeness, to betray thus the trust of his fellow Georgians and our own expectations!

We never did get any explanation, from him or anyone else, and to this day, when thinking about it, none of us can come up with a plausible explanation. But there it was.

## The Decision

All this went through my mind in a flash. Jacques also remembered that weird evening very well, but did not seem concerned, did not think it would affect the tour in any way:

"I would not worry. We are going on an official mission jointly sponsored by the French and Soviet culture ministries, I am sure that nothing bad will happen."

I finally told him that I needed time to think about it, and would call him back in a day or two. Of course I could get back to the piano and practice sufficiently to be able to accompany Jacques; of course I wanted to jump on the occasion to finally go to Georgia. But while for Jacques and the ballet company it would be a simple artistic tour, for Ethery, her son Tariel the stage manager, and for myself, it would be a deeply emotional voyage, for me even political. Then I had to take in consideration the upheavals taking place in Georgia, where the nationalistic fervor was increasing every day with demonstrations for freedom and secession from the Soviet Union, complete with waving the flag and symbols of the first republic.

Once in Georgia I would not belong to myself entirely, since I could not fail to represent my father the first president, the colony of exiles in Leuville and France, the independence lost the very year of my birth almost 70 years before. Thus, before giving my answer to Jacques, I had to consider that I would be somehow the ambassador of a past that until very recently seemed to be gone forever, but now appeared ready to be born anew in a recovered independence, what with the fall of the Berlin wall and the cracks in the Soviet monolith that threatened from all sides.

After due reflection I accepted Jacques' offer to join the tour for the shows in Moscow, Tbilisi, Kutaisi, and Yerevan, but with the condition that when the company would go back to Paris, I would return to Tbilisi as a private person and stay there a couple of months: at a time when deep political upheavals were promising to change Georgia, my presence would help to establish a link with the first republic, which had been slandered and ignored for so long. Also, since I was a college professor, I thought it would be highly interesting to give lectures in Tbilisi on the United States, about which the Georgians knew practically nothing.

My decision taken, I called Jacques back: — All right, I agree. Send me the documentation I need, and I'll get a visa here in New York. With my American passport, perhaps the Soviets won't make the connection with my father's name, or more probably, after all that time, they couldn't care less.

Indeed the Soviet visa turned out to be no problem, so that in September I flew to Paris to learn Jacques' songs and rehearse with him. I certainly needed that time to get my fingers and the musical part of my brain moving again!

Ethery and Jacques were the directors of a children's theater, *Le Théâtre du Jardin* located in the Botanical Gardens in Paris. It was a jewel of a small theater dedicated to present shows for grade-school children and introducing them to classical ballet through dance workshops  geared to their age-groups. It was very charming and was very successful.

Rehearsals for the new show lasted three weeks. I took advantage of this stay in Paris to spend time with my family and old friends with whom I had grown up in Leuville. Finally we left for Moscow, Ethery, Jacques and me by plane, the company with costumes, scenery and sundry paraphernalia by train: two and a half days! But they were all young and energetic, so they did not mind, and even enjoyed it a lot, I was told later. In Moscow we gave three shows, and then, finally, the day so long awaited was upon us: departure for Tbilisi.

Thus it was that I, son of President Noé Jordania, born in Paris after my parents were obliged to flee Georgia by the invading Red Army, after living 40 years in France, and then almost 30 years in the States, I was finally able to come to my ancestors' land, that very real Georgia which for me had so long remained a mysterious, mythical entity.

## Tbilisi, at Last!

As soon as the plane bringing us from Moscow touched ground at Tbilisi airport Tariel exclaimed: "At last! Here, we are home!" And it was absolutely true. All of a sudden, without transition, even before the plane doors opened, the atmosphere in the cabin felt immeasurably lighter: even though Georgia was still very much ruled from Moscow, we all had the strong feeling that we had left behind the Soviet Union with its ingrained suspicions, forbidden imperatives, bureaucratic obstacles, to arrive in a different country, that Georgia we did not know but that was deeply embedded in our heart, all three of us, son, grand-daughter and great-grandson of President Noé Jordania.

The arrival in Tbilisi was unforgettable! What a welcome! The officials, of course, but also so many Jordania and Pagava relatives, friends, admirers! We were invited and feted everywhere, official receptions, formal *supras* (banquets), and of course private dinners right and left. We were obliged to refuse many tempting invitations, because we had to rehearse and keep our energy for the stage. It goes without saying that the performances were a hit – the Opera House was packed every time!

We were so taken by it all that although I well knew that Georgia was going through a crucial period that would bring a total change to the local government in the near future, with the Communist Party, all-powerful for so long, in its death throes – no one foresaw the disintegration of the Soviet Union, which happened less than 12 months later officially on December 31, 1991 – knowing this, I still did not at all realize how much dislocation and hardship the process would bring about. In my defense I must say that most if not all Georgians had no inkling either. It was as if the struggle for free elections, the elections themselves, the boycott of the elections by some parties, all that would affect only the country's political leadership, and that everyday life would continue more or less as in the past. The big difference would be the breaking away from the Soviet Union, independence, the end of the Communist Party domination, and as a consequence a gradual opening to the West which could not fail to shortly bring prosperity. What blindness! But who could tell?

I will not dwell on this official period in Georgia. Simply note that after the shows in Tbilisi and Kutaisi we left for two performances in Yerevan. Then the troupe returned to Paris, and as for me, finally free, I took the train to Tbilisi.

---

# 11. TBILISI DIARY: Fall 1990
## *The Rise of Independent Georgia*

**Wednesday 30 October**

This morning we arrived by train to Tbilisi from Yerevan at 9.30 in the morning - 14.30 hours for 260 Kilometers! I must say I was well rested, too well, perhaps, since there was not much to do in the train but sleep. The bunks were fairly comfortable, and, in the morning, the attendant brought us strong tea, readymade with a lot of sugar. Upon arrival we went directly to Lika's place, she gave me the key to the studio, where I gratefully and happily made myself at home: the first time I was not living out of a hotel room in close to two months. I was to remain in that studio for almost six weeks, all by myself, and a most propitious time it was in that large space with almost all the comforts of home. Well, the telephone was, to say the least, most interesting in its erratic and unpredictable workings, hot water was conspicuous more by its absence than by its abundance, but these were but small drawbacks compared to the luxury of being in my own, private space.

In the afternoon, Kote came to see me to organize my series of lectures on American Civilization, and later we went for a walk in the mountains surrounding Tbilisi. This is one of the features I love here: you can start walking uphill right from downtown, and within perhaps 20 minutes you leave the city behind you and find yourself on paths meandering up the mountain. As you go up you may encounter a flock of sheep with its shepherd, a few cows contentedly munching on the vegetation, a couple of pigs rooting about, and perhaps one or two other persons wandering around. On that occasion, Kote and I went quite high up the hills, and turned back only because it was getting to be dark. The weather was lovely, dry and clear, not too hot, not too cold, and I felt such energy in my limbs that I had not known since a long time ago! It was as if going up those steep inclines pumped vigor into me, instead tiring me. So much so that Kote, who is 20 years younger than me, and professes to love exercising, asked me: "Do you hike great distances every day?"

In truth, I had practically not walked much ever since we went on tour.  But I felt great.  I am beginning to think there may be something to say for "natural" products:  all these vegetables that we are eating here are small, but they are grown naturally, organically, and taste delicious.  Georgians love to eat well, and their diet includes a lot of fruits and vegetables, prepared in a very delicious and, incidentally, healthy way. Their favorite cheese *is Suluguni*, similar to the greek Brinza, which seems to me to be made of skimmed milk, since while quite delicious, it does not feel fatty like a camembert or a goat cheese.  But if you are on a low salt diet, forget it:    the cheese is loaded with salt, probably for conservation, since refrigeration is still not widespread.    On our way back, we were stopped by a local who asked us if we had seen his cows.  He was looking for them to bring them back to his stable.  We told him that yes, we had seen four cows near the lake down below, and that they seemed to be going uphill.  That led to a discussion about the ways of cattle which I could but imperfectly follow.  But what amused me most was that there we were, right on top of a very busy city of 1,300,000 persons, with a lot of car traffic, and that cows and other animals could wander freely right in what was, in effect, an urban park.


**Thursday 1 November**

Today I did not have anything special on my agenda, so I got around to calling the young man who runs here the so-called Iberia news agency.  His name was given to me by Eduard Gudava, the former refusenik who was granted asylum in the States, and was director of the Center for Democracy in the USSR in Manhattan (now defunct). This young man, Zurab, turned out to be quite enthusiastic and very personable, and so were his associates: very refreshing after these people we kept meeting all the time in those *supras*, all so conventional, always repeating the same polite but boring ideas and sentiments. Yes, these young men are refreshing because they seem to be really aware of what's going on and do not hesitate to express their own ideas and interpretation of events here in Georgia.

Come to think of it, perhaps I am being unfair to our official hosts, who probably treated us as tourists and performers, which we were, and did not want to bother us with internal problems, but were only intent upon showing the best hospitality. Perhaps I am finally entering the real Georgia, now that I am on my own.

With Zurab, Guga, and a couple of other young men, we first went to a cafe nearby. We sat at a table where two other men were already seated — a common thing here, when there are no free tables. My escort started talking with the others, told them who I was, but they would not believe I was the son of Noe Jordania. "If he actually were the son of Noe Jordania, there would be a big deal, he would not be simply sitting in a cafe like that!" They even wanted me to show them some I.D., which I refused, explaining that in the US, first no one has an official paper like they do, called an Internal Passport, and that second, if they did not want to believe me, they were quite free to do so. I sometimes think that they were later embarrassed when they saw me on television, where my splendid face appeared more than once.

Later we of course went to a restaurant, of course only men, of course had a *supra*, with the difference that instead of a boring *tamada* (toast-master), expressing at great length the trite feelings and wishes that had been our fare so far, we were only five or six, with the owners of the restaurant joining us,

169

and discussed topics which are for me of great interest: current events, personalities, changing mores and patterns of society, all that in Georgian, yet, since the topics were concrete and specific, it was all real, comprehensible to me despite my limited knowledge of the language. They were all my kind of people, real democrats at heart, I think, even though their interpretation of this political stance may be quite different from what we are used to in the West. For the first time since I arrived in Georgia 6 weeks before, here were people really talking about issues, about the grave problems confronting the nation. Naturally, my new friends are in the opposition.

It seems that the elections in Georgia were won by Zviad Gamsakhurdia and his Round Table party, which received 70% of the votes, and that my friends call fascist.

They say that this majority is misleading, since the main opposition party boycotted the elections, and that many more people are against the Round Table than the polling numbers show. They also say that the good thing was that the communists were thrown out, but that the next step would be to get rid of the fascists, as represented by these people of the Round Table. Still the important is that there were free elections, the first in 70 years. People here are just not used to it, and they'll have to find their own way. We, from abroad, cannot do more than encourage them in following their own path.

### Monday 5 November

But back to the present. Kote, Lika, and naturally Tsira all came to pick me up and go to the Foreign Language Institute, for my first lecture on American Civilization. The lecture was very well received. There were perhaps 100 persons in the classroom, most of them students of English, and they seemed to understand me. I started with a personal

170

note, in response to questions: they all wanted to know where I grew up, how was our everyday life with my father and family in Paris, why I moved to America — a beautiful American girl found me in Spain, and brought me over" was my response, which elicited a lot of approving laughs. And that Sunday New York Times I lugged from the States proved its worth: it was a great success, and immediately set the tone. They could not understand how a newspaper would be that big and that wasteful. Indeed, I was told later: "If you had not shown us the size and weight of this paper, we would never have believed it!"

Towards the end of the lecture, I asked them to write down for me the subjects they were particularly interested in with the idea of integrating them in my twice-weekly lectures. They sent over a dozen questions. To my surprise, nine out of twelve wanted me to speak about religion in America! Upon reflection, though, it is not so astonishing: after 70 years of suppression and persecution of religion, it is no wonder that there is an upsurge. In fact, I was told that it is now a kind of fashion to get baptized.


**Wednesday 7 November**

Today I took a taxi to go to the Foreign Language Institute, where I had a lecture at 2 p.m. I mention this otherwise unremarkable fact because as we arrived to my destination, the taxi driver adamantly refused to take my money. I really tried to push money on him, telling him that after all it was his livelihood, to no avail. And it was not because of the Jordania name —at that time, I had not yet appeared on television, so people did not yet recognize me in the street —, no, it was simply because obviously I was a foreigner, and as such I was a *Stumari*, a guest: a sacred title in Georgia.

I can't think of any other country where such a courtesy would be extended, except perhaps Spain in the long-

171

ago post World War II period, before tourists started coming in droves. As for New York City, we all know that the quality of "foreigner" makes one fair game for any red-blooded taxi driver!

### Thursday 8 November

Yesterday was a historic day in Georgia. For the first time in 70 years, everybody went to work! There was no parade celebrating the October Revolution! For everybody here, it was a very great event, even though they lost a free day. But later it was announced that in compensation Friday would be a holiday, so all is well. There is a rumor that this year, also for the first time since 1921, Christmas would be a holiday! These, as I can see, are the most visible signs of change. But we are all waiting for the new, freely elected parliament to convene on November 15 to see what will be in store.

### Friday 9 November

I was scheduled for a recording session at the Museum of Literature — I thought such places were called libraries, but why not museum, after all? I met with Professor Givi Jordania at noon, on the steps of the University main building, and we proceeded to an office in the history department, where the video recording would take place. To my surprise, a whole slew of students, teachers, and other officials showed up, so many that they could not fit in that office. Quite a few people remained standing in the corridor, trying to hear what was going on.

Givi started the proceedings by introducing me. I then started talking, in French, and Givi translated into Georgian for everyone's benefit. I did not know that he knew French so well. The session lasted about one hour and a half. What they all wanted to hear were details about my father's life in exile, where we lived, how we lived, what did he do, whom did he see, and so on.

## Tbilisi Diary: Fall 1990

Some of the questions from the students seemed to me to be loaded politically, so I refused to answer them, saying that such issues were best left to historians. By and large, I thought that everything went very well, and I returned home for a well deserved rest.

### Thursday 15 November

This morning dawned as the historic first session of the new parliament. I went to a friend's house to watch, since my television is black and white, and with a very poor-quality picture; also, I preferred to be with Georgians who could help explain what was going on. His parents were also there, and some other friends came later in the day because a blackout took place in their neighborhood. We spent the day watching.

Zviad Gamsakhurdia was unanimously elected President of Parliament, as was expected, since his party won 70% of seats, the communists coming second with 25%, and the rest going to individuals. The new Parliament is to name ministers, modify the Constitution, adopt new laws, in short, effect all the changes necessary. Zviad's policy is to not yet declare independence, since it was seen by the example of Lithuania that such a move did not result in any particular progress, but to proclaim a transition period of two years towards a free Georgia.

Today's most emotional moments came toward the end. Parliament declared henceforth obsolete the Communist Georgian flag and national anthem, and restored the flag that was adopted by my father's government

173

in 1918: Bordeaux, with a black and a white band, symbolizing the blood spilled to defend the country, the times of slavery, and the times of freedom. It also restored the national anthem of that time, Dideba, and as a national symbol St. George, the patron saint of Georgia, but not the usual picture of the saint subduing the dragon, but rather of Saint George riding proud against a blue sky, upon which shine the seven planets of mythology standing for the traditional seven provinces of Georgia. And, to the applause of the multitude by that time assembled on the steps outside, the old communist flag was pulled down from all the government buildings, and the new/old one hoisted.

This must have been a really great emotional moment for all Georgians, who for the first time in practically everybody's life could see these symbols of freedom. As for me, what touched me was their emotion, not the symbols. After all, since I was born and raised in emigration, I had never known any other Georgian flag than this one, never heard any other national anthem but Dideba, never seen any other symbol than Saint George.

Parliament, and all the speakers, made a point that by reinstating these three objects they wanted to affirm the continuity of present-day Georgia with the years of independence, 1918-1921, when my father was President, and consider the 69 years of Communist rule as a long aberration.

One sad note: Sulkhanishvili did not make it. He was an old Georgian who lived in San Diego, USA, perhaps the last Georgian alive to have taken a leading part in the 1924 insurrection against the Bolshevists. He had been an officer then, and when it was clear the insurrection was not going to succeed, he went into exile, taking with him the flag of his unit: "One day," he swore, "this flag will fly again in my motherland." Some Georgians from here went to San Diego and brought him back to Tbilisi, him and the flag. But he died just 3 days before. At least, he had the joy of being back in his country for a short while, and his own flag was the actual one that was presented to Parliament.

Speaking of St. George: it is interesting to note that just about the same time, in New York, in the garden of the United Nations, was inaugurated with great fanfare a sculpture by the Soviet-Georgian sculptor Zurab Tsereteli, dedicated by the Soviet central government to the U.N. to mark the end of the cold war. This great work shows Saint George, on his horse, destroying a dragon made of parts of an American Pershing missile and parts of a Soviet nuclear missile.

I was told that in 1918, some wanted to adopt as the symbol of Georgia Prometheus, who the Greek legend says is chained on a rock of the Caucasus Mountains with a vulture tearing at his liver because he stole enlightment from the gods and gave it to mankind. But my father advised against it, because of the negative connotations, and that's how *Tsminda Georgi*, riding proud in a field of planets, came to become the symbol of this country

**Friday 16 November**

Today, I addressed Parliament. While we were watching the proceedings yesterday in my friend's house, I began to think to myself that my place also was there, in Parliament, since I represent the living link between free Georgia of 70 years ago, of which my father was president, and the new Georgia, with its attempt to re-establish continuity with that time. Before I expressed my view, however, his mother said it for me. They called someone, who called someone, and so the following morning I was brought to Parliament. We were given special passes, escorted inside, where we waited for the big man of the hour, Gamsakhurdia. When he appeared, I congratulated him, and he asked me to please wait until he

175

would call on me.      We dutifully sat in the aisles, while proceedings went on their way.  Already I could see curious glances toward me, not least from some of the Communist delegates, who happened to be seated near-by.

Then Zviad called upon Merab Costava's mother. Merab Costava was the undisputed leader of the independence movement, Gamsakhurdia and others being his lieutenants.  But Costava was killed in an automobile accident just about 18 months ago.  There is suspicion of foul play, but nothing concrete.  He was then about 60 years old.  The fact is, had he been alive, most Georgians would have united behind him.  As it is, while the Round Table, under Gamsakhurdia, won the official elections and dominates Parliament, a rival organization, also elected, sprang up:   Congress, led by Chanturia.  Well, I suppose it would have been too much for the Georgians to present a common front:  it sure as hell is not in their temperament!

Merab Costava's mother spoke.  She was a frail lady in her late eighties, yet spoke clearly and well, I gather, and was much applauded.  Then Zviad called on me.  He said: "And now, as a symbol of continuity for our country, I offer you Noe Jordania son, Redjeb."  As I walked up the aisle toward the podium, all the delegates stood up, applauding.  I must say it was perhaps the most significant moment of my life, yet I was probably too numb to feel much.  I walked that aisle slowly, looking straight-ahead, climbed to the podium, and spoke, with hesitations and long pauses.  In fact, I did much better at the Opera in Tbilisi and Kutaisi!

I did not say anything of any great import, but it was not what I was saying that counted, but the fact that here I was, in Parliament, talking to the delegates:  a fact which would have been totally unthinkable just a few weeks before! And indeed this is how it was taken and cheered not only in Parliament but in the whole country, since the session was televised, and the highlights, of which I was one, were broadcast over and over again.

"I am proud to be here with you in these historic days," I said, rather haltingly, speaking in Georgian."Seventy years ago my father and his associates were obliged to go into exile, when the Bolshevik army invaded our country. I was born abroad, lived 40 years in France, almost 30 years in the United States. And at long last, the greatest wish of my life came to pass: here I am in Georgia, my own country. Now I have a second wish: I wish to shake the hand of the second President of Free Georgia [tremendous applause]. The path will be hard, there are many obstacles, but I am convinced we shall prevail!" And with that, I punched the air with my right fist closed, to a long ovation that lasted until I was back in my seat.

Recess was then called. All kinds of people came to shake my hand. The all-soviet television network interviewed me – the whole interview was aired at the midnight news spot-photographers asked me to repeat my punching gesture, which they had missed. In short, I was now famous, and would be henceforth famous in the whole country, not least because the following week television chose to show the footage they had filmed at the opera, showing me playing solo my compositions, Jacques singing with me accompanying, excerpts from Ethery's ballet, and finally, at length, the curtain calls, focusing on Tariel, Ethery's son, Noé Jordania's great-grandson, Ethery his grand-daughter, and myself. Three generations of Noé Jordania's descendants, together and collaborating on the stage!

Among those who came to shake my hand in Parliament was one social-democrat, who was not a deputy. Social-democracy was the party of my father. Now eclipsed, it had an honorable following in the twenties, with luminaries such as the Welshman Lloyd George, war-time prime minister of Great Britain, the Belgian Vandevere, the German Karl Kautsky, and many more. Free Georgia was considered as the first Social Democrat country, and, in 1920, played host to an international congress of social-democrats, with the participation of all these important figures.

Among the many parties that competed in the 1990 first free elections was the newly-reconstituted social-democrat party. But not a single candidate was elected. Nevertheless they affirm the future is theirs in Georgia, and are planning Noe Jordania commemorative institutions, such as a museum in Lanshkhuti, in a reconstituted Jordania house, and one in Tbilisi, where he used to live, in a great building, well conserved, where a bank is now housed. These new social-democrats labor under a grave handicap: the word "socialism" is anathema to most Georgians, nay, to most Soviet people, attached as it has been for 70 disastrous years to the brand of so-called communism that subjugated those unhappy people for so long. These new social democrats of course wanted my support, but I told them that I did not feel it was proper at this stage for me to participate in the political life of a country which, after all, I hardly know.

### Saturday 17 November: Batumi

Friday evening, as planned, I took the train to Batumi, a port-city on the Black Sea: 14 hours for 350 Kilometers. Even the Long Island Railroad is way faster, never mind the TGV or the Japanese bullet-trains!

My old friend Thina and a group of people were waiting for me at the Batumi station. I had no idea who they were, but they did appear to be very excited and wanted immediately to do things. Thina prevailed upon them to give me some time to refresh myself, and we went to her apartment. In fact, we walked, since it was really very close, so close that we got there before my luggage, which someone was bringing in a car, because it had to detour through one-way streets.

Again I was struck by the contrast between the outside and inside of the buildings. Outside, the courtyard, entrance, staircase are rather derelict-looking, with chunks of cement missing here and there, ruts and potholes in the ground, occasional steps caved in. Inside, Thina's apartment was bright and cheerful, with good solid furniture, everything in excellent taste and good condition. Although some compare this state of affairs with what exists in certain projects here in the US, where the public parts are really awful, with garbage, rats, and smells of urine all over, in contrast with some of the apartments which are fairly well kept inside, the comparison would be misleading. In the Soviet Union, yes, the outside is kind of neglected, since it does not belong to anyone, and the janitors paid to take care of it do like everybody does here: the minimum possible. (How does the anecdote go: They pretend to pay us, and we pretend to work?)

Yet there is no willful damaging and mistreating. No smell of urine, no garbage floating all over, and, as far as one can tell no or very little drugs or crime. The buildings are wide open for anyone to come in, even though the apartments are kept locked like everywhere else. Yet people complain and say that crime is indeed increasing in worrisome proportions. To which I reply: "Well, you wanted freedom? Crime also is a manifestation of freedom!"

The situation reminds me of Spain years ago: under Franco, cities were reputed to be indeed very safe. There was little crime, one could wander the streets at all hours of the day and night, and the most active branch of police was the political one, which was very active indeed. And then, as society evolved, personal freedom increased, and finally Franco died, the dictatorship being replaced with a democratic society, robberies, muggings, and crime in general increased dramatically, to reach the level of neighboring countries such as France and Italy, all of which, incidentally, are way below the crime-level of the U.S. Georgia was not yet there, and perhaps will never reach even those relatively moderate levels, since it is a small country with very strong family ties,

179

but for the people here the upsurge is frightening, and will no doubt last as long as the economic situation does not improve.

At the moment, there is no sign of betterment, on the contrary, it goes from bad to worse, and soon will be awful - yet remains better in Georgia that in most of the Soviet Union, in part thanks to the climate that permits better and more extensive crops, in part thanks to the entrepreneurial and individualistic characteristics of the Georgians:  if free enterprise has a hold anywhere, it's in this country.

Batumi is the capital of Adjara.  In the Soviet system, Adjara is officially an autonomous republic yet remains part of Georgia. It has its own government, however, but everybody here speaks Georgian.  The main difference is that there are a lot of Moslem Georgians here, which explains why many here voted Communist in the recent free elections:  the other political parties emphasized their Christianity, while the communists remained officially neutral, a great progress after 70 years of actively repressing religion. Historically, though, there never has been an autonomous Adjara.  It was always part of Georgia, even after the Turks grabbed most of the region's area, which used to extend all the way to Trebizond, three hours away by car.

Since Adjara has its own government, I was dutifully taken to Government House, where I was received by the Assistant Prime Minister, a very nice woman who proceeded to vaunt the beauties of her province. I did not quite grasp why I had to go see that person, since I took my visit to Thina to be a private, personal visit to an old friend.  Little did I understand then the power and attraction of my name, particularly since I had been on TV the day before, addressing parliament.  Yet, Thina explained: "If you had come here a week ago, before the new parliament convened and changed things around, these same people who are making such a fuss about you would probably have ignored you, they would still have been afraid!"

## Tbilisi Diary: Fall 1990

In the strange ways that Soviet society functions, the man who in practice took charge of me and showed me around was the President of the Dramaturgist Society, Alexandre Tshkheidze. Somehow that position entitled him to an official car with chauffeur, and, presumably, an expense account. He seemed to know everybody, and kept introducing me — or showing me off? — to a lot of people, meantime taking photos and videotaping the encounters.

I did not mind him, since he was a very congenial and enthusiastic man of perhaps sixty years of age, with grey hair, rather stout, and a very inquisitive manner which could have been annoying if it did not obviously correspond to a keen interest. He quizzed me mercilessly about the exact day and hour of my birth and other family matters, and engaged in long historical reflections and calculations the point of which escaped me. Until he declared triumphantly: "Well, as far as I can make out, you are truly from Batumi! Yes, your parents' last few days before they left for exile were spent here, in that house overlooking the harbor — which he showed me — and that's where you were conceived!" A theory he went on expounding to all and sundry during my stay in Batumi, to my embarrassment. But I got used to it, after all, and when they insisted on filming me following in the footsteps of my father's last days in his country, in February 1921, I saw no reason to object to anything: that's the price one pays for "celebrity."

He may be right about my conception, for all I know. Yet I have my pet theory, which better accounts for my love of boats and of the sea, a feeling no one in my family shares to the slightest degree: I was conceived on the liner that took my parents into exile, and that sailed from Batumi on the Black Sea to Marseilles in southern France, a week's journey in those days. But in any case I liked Batumi very much, with its balmy weather, palm trees, large gardens and promenades, old men sipping Turkish coffee on the harbor, and the overall air of decayed gentility of a spa bypassed by modern life.

In the afternoon, I was taken on the road to Turkey to join the throng waiting for the king. The king in question was Solomon II, last king of Georgia, who was forced into exile when the Russians occupied Georgia in 1783, and died and was buried in Turkey in the early 1800's. His casket was being returned to Georgia that day, and we all waited in front of an old fortification outside Batumi, of which only the crenellated walls and massive gates remained.

There were a lot of people, many in national costumes, a gigantic "new" Georgian flag hanging across the gate, and many other picturesque banners and pennants gaily waving in the sunny breeze. And lo and behold: a troop of horse-mounted honor guards in national costume, with pennants flying, the heel of the staff pushed into the right boot, came thundering down the road. A wonderful sight, better than at the movies! So we waited and waited. After a while, nothing happening, we went back to Batumi, and rightly so: we learned later that the King finally arrived only after 10 p.m.

**Sunday 18 November**

This morning I went out by myself for a walk through the city. I enjoyed my morning stroll, for once alone free to go where my fancy took me. The weather was clear and sunny, the air balmy, and the Black Sea just a few blocks away. Gardens and alleys meander alongside the shore, but the beach is not too appealing, since it is made of pebbles, not sand. There were very few people around at that time of the morning, yet I was recognized several times, and had to refuse offers to escort me wherever I was going. "Nowhere," I would explain in my broken Georgian."I am just walking around, looking." I did learn however that the king had finally arrived, and that he was lying in state in a church nearby, before continuing to Tbilisi, where he would be reunited with other kings of Georgia in the mausoleum.

*Tbilisi Diary: Fall 1990*

I went back to Thina's, dressed in more formal clothes than my early morning blue jeans and sweatshirt, and, with two of her friends, ambled over to that church. I wanted to see the casket, and take a couple of photos. I had forgotten that I was a media personality! The church was crowded, with a lot of people spilling outside on the patio and the street. Hardly had I entered the church, jockeying for a view of the casket, that I was led aside, surrounded by mostly older women while TV cameras focused on me, and I was here and there interviewed by I don't know who they were, but many persons. I was even asked to join the choir and sing, or pretend to sing, Georgian religious songs for a minute or two, while the cameras took everything in. Incidentally, these Georgian church songs, as most Georgian folksongs, are polyphonic, with at least three voices, and are indeed beautiful in their stately progress.

After that I was again surrounded by mainly women, jostling each other and asking for autographs. I was told later that two women even got into a real fight, each accusing the other of not letting her come close enough! The TV people wanted to continue my interview there and then, but I told them that it would be more convenient the following day. I also declared that since Adjara is a mostly Moslem country, and since I had already been in a church, I wanted next to visit a mosque. Well, that visit to King Solomon turned out to be a bit on the busy side. I never did get to see the casket, except a slight glimpse through the throng, did not take any photos, yet it was strangely satisfying in its own way.

We then took off for Lanshkhuti for the emotional reunion with the land of my ancestors that I related at the beginning of these memoirs.


**Tuesday 20 November: Tbilisi**

I arrived from Batumi this morning at 8 a.m., after a peaceful night in the train. I must confess that I still don't

183

know how to grease palms. Since everybody seems to give money to attendants on the train and in other places, I wanted to do the same. I folded 30 rubles in my hand, and tried to give it discretely to the *dizhurnaia*, the lady in charge of the 1st class sleeper. But she looked at it, did not take it, and said: "What's that for?" I insisted: "For you." She still didn't take it: "But I did not do anything special." "Well, it's in case," I said. I had to keep pressuring her to take that money, which she did finally, but half-heartedly, almost making me feel I had somehow trespassed! Even though I know damn well it is not only done, but one had better do it for practically everything. Was her reluctance genuine? Was it because she actually did not do anything special for me, except perhaps for giving me tea, which she does anyhow? Or was it because she knew who I was, son of the President?

Something good came out of that episode. The following day, I had to come back to the train to send Thina a blank videotape, so that the Adjara TV could make me a copy of the program they had put together of my visit to Batumi. Things are so scarce that even the official TV station did not have a good spare tape for me! And of course, sending anything like that by mail was out of the question, hence the train. The same *dizhurnaia* was there. Of course she recognized me right away. "Are you already going back," she asked, surprised. "No," I said," I am sending this small package to Mrs. Sardjveladze. Will you ..." "Oh, I know the lady very well. I'll take care of it. And please nothing else is needed," she added forcefully, referring to what was in her view the unearned tip I gave her the night before. That was, to remind you, 30 rubles, or three days wages— one and a half dollars.

Coming back to my arrival in Tbilisi: there is a subway at the train station, but, since I had luggage, I decided to take a taxi. I approached one: nothing doing. Another: same thing. Another: the driver started to say "no," when a passerby yelled at him: "Take him! Don't you recognize him? He is Noé Jordania's son!" At which the driver did take me home, first ascertaining however that I would pay him the 10 rubles he demanded — an outrageous price by local standards, yet only 50 cents for me. Well, that was kind of reassuring to encounter a typical taxi driver, quite worthy of his New York counterparts!

Later in the day I gave my fourth lecture on American Civilization at the Foreign Language Institute. Today's subject was Entertainment and the Arts. Students and professors, as usual, showed themselves keenly interested. I showed them the New York TV guide, and counted the channels: over 40! They couldn't believe it! I also showed them the New York Times Sunday Arts section: so many things happening in just one city!

But what mostly fascinated them was the Foundation system in America. They could not understand why private persons would give money for philanthropic and artistic reasons, a thing unheard of until very recently in Georgia. I tried to explain the Income Tax deductions system, by which it could actually be financially advantageous for a wealthy person or company to give away money, or so it used to be. I am not sure it is still the case after Reagan's Income Tax reforms.

The National Endowment for the Arts they could well understand, since it resembles somewhat what happens here. But when I attempted to describe the recent brouhaha about so-called "pornographic" art, they didn't follow me at all. "Why should the government give money for such disgusting things," they kept wondering, referring to the Oglethorpe exhibition and other controversial artists. I explained the best I could the fear of censorship, and how this would be contrary to the principle of free speech. They politely agreed, but I could see that at bottom they were all for Senator Jesse Helms on that subject.

Incidentally, recently some Georgians and Armenians in this country did give considerable sums of money after the earthquakes and other catastrophic events, but they did it anonymously, and nobody, at least officially, knows who they are. The reason being that they are afraid of being accused of profiteering and black marketing, since how else could they have amassed such huge sums to give away? A reasoning which, I must say, does have some merit. After all, weren't our first philanthropists, the Rockefellers, Vanderbilts, Goult etc., nicknamed with good reason the Robber Barons?

**Thursday 22 November**

Law school students asked me to give a lecture on the legal system in the United States. I carefully explained that in no way was I was a jurist, and therefore whatever I could explain would be from the point of view of an ordinary citizen. But they insisted: "We know almost nothing about the legal realities in the United States. Anything you can tell will interest us a lot. So I complied.

They were close to two hundred crowded into a large classroom. My translator — I was speaking in English — was a young student who had made several trips to the United States and knew the language very well. In fact, as soon as I started talking, he embarked on a simultaneous translation that got everybody confused because, since there was no headphone system, everybody heard both languages simultaneously! I was obliged to stop talking, and, while complimenting him on his expertise, asked him to wait for me to pause before translating.

I explained as best I could the American system, from the Supreme Court to the traffic judge. What surprised the students most is that so many judicial positions are awarded through elections, not meritocracy, such as municipal judges, district attorneys, and many others. "But this opens the way for plenty of corruption, no?" they asked. They were greatly astonished when I explained to my knowledge, although there are many abuses, overall the system does not work too badly or at least it is generally accepted. In the United States the rational is that, since those judges are elected, they have to behave themselves, otherwise they will not be reelected!

The students were fascinated with the system of appointment for life of many high judicial positions, in which the President of the United States proposes candidates, and the Senate confirms or not, as the case may be. "How can the Senate *not* approve someone appointed by the President? " they wondered. When I told them that politics were in full play in these appointments, they asked: "But are there such great differences between Democrats and Republicans?" Not to go into details — it was late — I simply replied: "When Democrats are in power, their policies tend to help the poor and the middle class. When the Republicans are in power the opposite is true, the money goes to the rich, which is to say to those who do not need more. "(That was in 1990. In re-reading these lines in 2011, this trend has been pushed to the extreme. The Republican far right has taken over, with the result that 50 years of social progress is being dismantled, corporations influence government policy to an unmatched degree, the rich get vastly richer, and the barrier between state and religion is under assault.)

After the conference itself, the students asked me many questions about my family, on emigration. And one of them asked: "Your father was not president of Georgia, was he? He was <u>only</u> the Head of the Council of Ministers, no?"!

There it was. Again, this attempt to minimize the importance of my father that remains for me incomprehensible — because it showed very well that the question was not a simple issue of semantics, but rather an assertion.

It was only slowly that I realized the profound ignorance, even hostility that many Georgians showed about my father and the first Georgian republic. If many knew only his name, and that in a manner vaguely derogatory, that was hardly surprising after more than three generations of Soviet propaganda. But among those who should have more information, intellectuals and politicians for example, the manifest negativity towards this period was indeed unexpected.

It is true that the first independence was a short episode, considering only the sidereal time and not the subjective human time. But all Western historians, without exception, recognize its high degree of success despite the enormous difficulties of the time, and the enormous influence that these three years of independence exercised over the development of the country. All major institutions that make a country were created then, but the most important by far is the simple fact that for the first time in centuries Georgia was united, independent and truly democratic.

One of the most surprising facets of this hostility is the fact that even the title of President is denied to my father. Many Georgians insist that he was "only" prime minister, not president, in part, some say, because Zviad Gamsakhurdia wanted at all costs to be the "first" president of Georgia. Their assertion is based on the fact that my father was not elected by popular vote but rather by the cabinet and parliament, as was customary in France at the time, for example, or today in the Czech Republic, among others.

Note that in the United States, contrary to popular belief, the president is not elected directly by universal suffrage. Americans vote for a board of electors, and these, in turn, vote for a president. The result is that a president can be elected even if he lost the popular vote. Also, in theory nothing prevents the board of electors to elect as president a person entirely different from the one chosen by the voters.

As for my father, all my life I had always heard him referred to as President. In all documents and newspaper articles I had ever seen, it was the same. Thus I was rather taken aback when, in Georgia, his status was questioned. Another rather puzzling fact: while the flag, coat of arms, and national anthem of the first republic were revived and adopted by the new Georgia, as well as its constitution, I never heard any of the new politicians in power publicly mention any of the great men and women who were the actual creators of the 1918 independence. It would take me time to understand the phenomenon. (See **Post-Script**: *Reflections on My Georgias*).

**Friday 23 November**

It looks like my project for a Summer English Language Institute is going forward.

For some time I had been thinking about what could I personally do in order to help Georgia. One thing was clear: what Georgians most want at this time is to escape the strictures of the stifling Soviet system and open themselves to the West, in general, and to the United States in particular. So that I thought the best way for me was to draw upon my university-teaching experience and my familiarity with the American system to recruit volunteer teachers in the US and bring them to Tbilisi. I was very sure I could do the recruiting, but did not know how to find the proper location here, recruit students, and in general how to organize the program in Tbilisi.

I discussed the situation with Lika, since she is very well connected, and also with Kote, in his capacity as English teacher in the Foreign Language Institute in Tbilisi. And sure enough they came through with a solution.

Thus it is that this afternoon we went to see the president of the trade-unions, Petre Chkheidze (Yes, they have unions in the Soviet Union, even though the government owns everything and is supposedly run by the proletariat!). Petre was very receptive. He suggested that the Institute could take place in the unions' facilities located on the banks of Tbilisi Sea, a man-made lake just 20 minutes away from Tbilisi proper. That same afternoon he took us there to visit.

We couldn't have a more suitable location: they have everything, including a small hotel, several classrooms, a restaurant, and even a beach down below – no mean asset, considering we would be there in the height of summer.

So it was decided: Petre would provide the facilities, Kote the academic organization, and Lika the overall organization, including meeting us in Moscow to bring us to Georgia.

Of course the whole thing concluded with a modest banquet: some 20 persons loosely connected to the organization plus the four of us, a good dozen courses in the Georgian manner, lots of wine, and three-hour worth of toasts, Petre being the Tamada (toastmaster).

I shall be leaving for Paris, then New York the day after tomorrow. This first trip to the country of my ancestors has proven to be enormously fulfilling, and I am already looking forward to coming back next summer with a group of American ESL teachers for another great sojourn.

---

# 12. DIARY: One Year Later
### Decline and Fall of President Gamsakhurdia ...
### and of the Soviet Union

**August 19, 1991**

Our first warning that something very important had happened came when I turned on the morning news: the Russian TV and radio programs were all playing the same solemn classical music! "Gorbachev is dead", was the first thought that came to mind.... It is only upon arriving at the classroom building that we learned what happened.

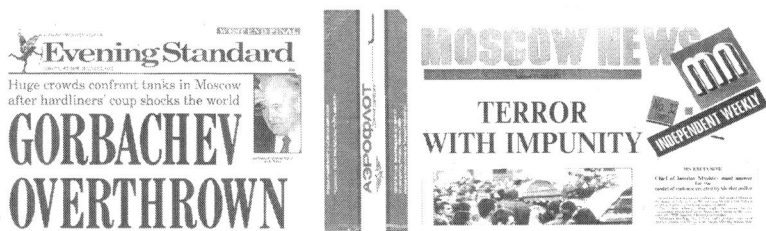

The weather was as usual wonderful, sunny but not too hot, with a light cool breeze from the mountains to the North. Down below already bathers were crowding the lake shores, where we were in the habit of going swimming after classes in the afternoon. Contrasting with the peaceful surroundings, our students were milling around in the patio, heatedly discussing the events. They told us that in Moscow a committee of eight had taken over in order to "save" the Union, that Gorbachev was under house arrest — nobody quite believed this—, that martial law had been proclaimed, and that all para-governmental militias were ordered disbanded. They also said that the Georgian president Zviad Gamsakhurdia had broadcast an appeal to the population urging everyone to remain calm and proceed as usual, and ordering the recently formed Georgian National Guard

191

dissolved "to avoid any clashes with the Soviet military", a decision for which he was roundly criticized. "How could our president obey so meekly this new bunch in Moscow? He could have at least waited a few hours before ordering our national guard dissolved!" many students commented. Others defended Zviad: "He is trying to avoid bloodshed. Don't you know there are 50,000 well-armed Soviet troops in Tbilisi? Do you want a repetition of April 9?" [On April 9, 1989, a contingent of Russian MVD elite troops of the Dzerzhinsky Division attacked peaceful Georgian demonstrators with poison gas and sharpened shovels, killing twenty and maiming many more.]

"That may be so, but Zviad got elected president on a platform of independence and non-obedience to Moscow. How can he cave-in so fast?" And the discussion went on and on.

As far as Gorbachev was concerned, however, the consensus was that he fully deserved what happened. In the whole Soviet Union Gorby is held in very low esteem, contrary to the West where he is seen as a great man. The reason is simple: since Perestroika started six years ago, goods have every year become scarcer and scarcer, and have now virtually disappeared from government stores.

"Do you think Gorbachev is really sick? Or did they kill him?" asked another student. "In the old times, he would certainly have been 'disappeared'; but now? I don't think they have the guts."

We are a group of nine Americans teaching an intensive ESL summer course in Tbilisi, capital of the Republic of Georgia. The program is sponsored by the Georgian Trade-Unions and takes place in their Educational Center. The site is magnificent: the Center is located on a bluff overlooking the Tbilisi Sea, a 10-mile long man-made reservoir surrounded by mountains, where swimming and boating are permitted. The city is but 20 minutes away, but the lake's waters are pristine, as there are no buildings on its shores except for our compound and a small hotel. The only sizeable town near-by is located below the lake level, on the hillside.

The Educational Center includes two classroom buildings, two small hotels, and a restaurant. A footpath leads directly down from the terrace to the beach, some 80 feet below. When we arrived on July 14, one of the buildings was occupied by the militia — that's the town police. But in August a contingent of National Guardsmen arrived, and we were told that at the end of our program the whole compound would be turned over to them. Already bulldozers are leveling an adjacent field, getting it ready for drills and exercises. Perhaps two dozen army vehicles are stationed here, and more arrive every day. A great plus is that now a gasoline truck comes once a week to re-supply the guard and our Georgian colleagues and students who have cars take advantage of the situation. It is so difficult to get gas in the city that often people have to wait in line for 24 hours or more!

This Georgian National Guard is composed of draftees who refuse to serve in the Soviet forces, where conditions are atrocious and minority kids, including Georgians, Armenians, Azeris and others are subject to extremes of hazing often leading to mutilation or death. Many smaller republics, besides Georgia, created their own national guard: The Baltic States, Armenia, Moldavia, and others. All of these formations are considered illegal by the central government, and were ordered immediately dissolved by the coup leaders.

It is rather amusing that the Soviet Army has a camp right across the road. There have been a few incidents with the Russian soldiers, who are all around 20-years old, like draftees anywhere. Once a drunken soldier climbed a drain pipe to the second-story balcony where our rooms are, and proceeded to dismantle a window to force his way inside even though one of our teachers was right there, scared out of his wits! The soldier was promptly chased away, but in the morning we discovered that the American flag that was flying at the main entrance had been stolen. Another time some Russian soldiers climbed on top of the classroom building, kicked in a glass door, sustaining some wounds in the process, bashed in other doors and smashed tape-recorders and other equipment, leaving a trail of blood throughout! The following day Soviet officers came to examine the damage, which they eventually made good. What happened to the culprits I do not know. We were also told that in town there occurred a few incidents between Soviet soldiers and civilians, and that Georgian National guardsmen are now patrolling the streets to help avoid further clashes.

That August 19, classes were as usual over at 2.30 p.m. Nothing more was known about events in Moscow. Some of our American teachers were getting quite worried, not because of the situation here in Georgia, but rather because they were scheduled to leave for the States that very week, and the road to America goes through Moscow! Our Georgian friends were promising they would do everything to get them on their way — no mean feat in itself since very few planes were flying from Tbilisi in the best of cases, because of the acute fuel shortage. But of course they had no control over the situation at Sheremetivo international airport in Moscow, 1500 miles away.

After class, everyone dispersed. I opted to go to town to see what if anything was happening there. When I left at three p.m. everything was calm, the national guardsmen and their equipment were all over the place doing nothing, as usual, the militia lolling around their building. Two hours later, when I returned, not a trace of them remained: not a truck, not a soldier, not a militiaman. Some said the boys' mothers came and dragged them home. Others said that the guard refused to obey Gamsakhurdia's order to disband, and went into hiding in the mountains. Only later we would learn that both versions were right. Part of the guardsmen just went home, but another contingent, 15,000 in all, actually retreated into the mountains under the direction of their commander, general Tengiz Kitovani. They would later join the political groups demonstrating against President Gamsakhurdia, whom they accused of having sold out to Moscow.

In the evening we watched the Russian TV broadcast of the coup leaders' press conference. It proved most interesting not so much because of the questions and answers, but rather because of the style and the feelings it conveyed. Only six of the leaders were present. Missing were Kryuchkov and Yasov, heads of the KGB and the ministry of defense, no doubt too busy organizing to lose time with a silly public relations exercise.

The questions dealt mostly with the whereabouts and condition of Gorbachev. The responses, delivered in a monotonous, dead voice, kept repeating: he is sick, unable to fulfill his duties, that's why we had to take over —an evident untruth that they obviously thought would be accepted if repeated often enough. The reporter's questions were polite and not very probing, except for one young woman: she phrased her questions in a way that was extremely critical of the coup leaders, by doing so risking her life, as we thought, or at least severe retribution. She was extremely nervous, twisting her hands, twirling her hair, fidgeting.... But she did say what no one else said, and we all admired her for it.

That afternoon, we heard that Bush had expressed "grave concern", a milksop statement that he redeemed later by joining France, Great Britain, Germany, and most other nations except Libya in condemning the coup and calling for an immediate reinstatement of Gorbachev. As for President Gamsakhurdia, he declared only that events in Moscow were not of any concern to Georgia, and called for immediate international recognition of Georgian independence, giving as his reason that events had shown how unworthy of leadership the Russian-dominated central government proved to be. [Georgia is the very first Soviet republic to have overwhelmingly voted for independence in a referendum pointedly held on April 9, 1991, the second anniversary of the 1989 massacre.]

The following morning I tried to reach President Gamsakhurdia, Vice-President Assatiani, or other members of the government, to no avail. Total confusion seemed to prevail. If the coup succeeded, it was clear that central control would be imposed anew. I can well picture all the middle level officials busily searching for their communist party card, which they had discarded a year ago.

I wanted to use whatever influence I may have had to try to impress on the Georgian officials that the proper way to act, the only way that would give Georgia some stature in Western eyes, would be to send a statement deploring the coup, thereby joining the world's chorus of condemnation. In fact, the return of Gorbachev was certainly in the Georgian national interest, given the dictatorial actions of the coup leaders. At least with Gorbachev, there was the possibility of dialogue.

Not only did Zviad not understand that elementary fact, but he gave an interview to CNN in which he declared that the so-called coup was nothing but a put-up job, that Gorby had orchestrated the whole thing because his popularity was slipping fast, and by presenting himself as a victim he hoped to regain his lost prestige. I still remember the unbelieving look of the CNN interviewer, her eyes opening wide, leaning forward flabbergasted upon hearing that declaration.

Even at the time such an interpretation was far from credible, and if by chance it were true it was certainly not the time and place to present it to the world. From then on President Gamsakhurdia lost a great deal of credibility in the West, to the great detriment of Georgia. But most of his die-hard partisans believed him, they still believe him months later, even though nothing transpired that could show collusion. Quite the contrary. Two of the coup leaders committed suicide, the others are in jail awaiting judgment, Gorbachev's prestige and authority are at an all-time low and further eroding everyday, and the many books and accounts published since the coup show not a hint of hanky-panky.

That same Tuesday morning we watched from our compound what looked like a Soviet military buildup. It so happened that our lake was under the flight path from the airport towards Russia, since the surrounding hills and tall mountains funnel the wind and preclude other directions. We thus always knew if there were planes to Moscow. But that day we could see army helicopter after helicopter flying low to the airport, engines laboring hard, and going back higher and faster. They were obviously shuttling in equipment and troops, and returning for more. We lost count after some 250 flights. The students told us that the same kind of military build-up took place just before the April 9 massacre. It sure looked and sounded ominous, but this time around nothing untoward happened.

By Wednesday it was already clear that the coup had

failed. We spent a good part of the day watching Russian TV. What made it clear for us was not so much what was happening and what was said, but rather what was shown: if the coup had succeeded never would we have seen Yeltsin, the crowds in Moscow hemming in soldiers and tanks, ordinary people openly stating their views ... and when the following day the Russian —not Soviet—parliament convened, the procedures, speeches, discussions, resolutions, coupled with the clear visual impact of it all, amounted to such an intense drama that even those of us who didn't know a word of Russian were absolutely fascinated.

What with CNN, the networks, the many correspondents roaming at will during this period, it is most probable that in the Western world people were better informed than we who were inside the country. But on another level we were much closer to the pulse of events just by being there, even though Tbilisi is 1500 miles away from Moscow. No amount of reading or viewing can ever replace a direct personal experience: to be within the political and cultural entity where the events take place, regardless of proximity, offers a direct gut feeling that no amount of information at distance can replace. Thus for me, being in Tbilisi during that time put me inside the emotional sphere of the upheaval, and gave me insights and understandings at a level not accessible to those witnessing the same events at a remove, even though they may have had access to more and more accurate news.

In all the turmoil, we managed to send to Moscow Sue Davis, one of our teachers, with the only plane that left that day. We later heard she caught without problem her plane connection to the States. In fact during all this time Sheremetivo airport functioned as efficiently as ever ... which is not saying much. But there was no disruption of international traffic. Yet at the time we didn't know that.

Two of our teachers who were supposed to leave Friday morning, got very nervous about it all. They complained bitterly not only about the planes and the situation, but in general because of the lack of information and the frustration of not knowing in advance what was going to happen. Americans are used to making plans, to foresee the immediate future with some precision.

"We never know what's happening," they complained to our Georgian hosts. "You never tell us anything, everything is always a surprise. You take us here and there without notice, without saying what it's all about. We want to be treated as adults, not children! We want to be told things, we want to know about difficulties, projects, plans, timetables, to learn in advance about the negative as well as the positive!"

But in the USSR things are quite different. I felt for them because even I, with my better cultural understanding and command of the language, was often frustrated. It is not that the Georgians were hiding anything. Rather, it is a phenomenon of the Soviet world that no one can say what will happen until it happens, so why bother speculating? In addition, our hosts have an understandable dislike of saying negative things: "Why say this or that is not possible, when for all we know it might come to pass at the very last minute? Better wait and see ... " In other words: stay loose and roll with the punches.

That's precisely what is hard for most Westerners, who are raised to impose some sort of arbitrary order on life and to expand the present so as to include the future: foresee, plan ahead, set money aside for contingencies, weigh the consequences. We are all brainwashed to the point that part of us is always on what is to come, thus loosing the acuity of the present moment which it seems we cannot bear if we do not have a fair idea of the future.

This is not so in other cultures that we term

"primitive", this is not so either for some people at certain levels of our own society, whom we call "shiftless" and "improvident". And this is not so in Soviet society, in part because the State is supposed to take care of all, and in part because it is generally useless to make definite plans since no one knows if they will be realizable.

What is the sense of planning to go shopping on your free day, for instance, since goods become available without rhyme or reason? Everything here takes 100 times longer than in the West, as communications are totally unreliable, and people are never where they are supposed to be or have not done what they are supposed to, because they too face the same difficulties.

This was very frustrating for our American teachers, even though they always ended up being taken care of generously and even extravagantly: "If my Georgian friends come visiting in the States, there is no way I can reciprocate to that degree!" exclaimed Andrew, expressing the common feeling.

In Georgia, guests are sacred. Everything is done for them, regardless of expense. The phrase *"Too much is not enough!"* rightly describes the Georgian brand of hospitality. In our case, in addition, was the fact that teachers and professors are highly respected. And our students, by and large, came from well-to-do, even wealthy families.

Yes, even over there, there are wealthy people! How it works, I do not know, but there it is, even without black-market or mafia activities. Tuition for our 6-week course was 1500 rubles, way above the head of most Soviet citizens. [As an example, a very high salary was 800 rubles a month at that time.] And then our program was considered very prestigious: it was the very first time in history that a group of real Americans were in Georgia teaching their own language and culture.

Some of the students were very well-to-do. They thought nothing of inviting our teachers to a week-end on the seaside or in the mountains, paying for train, plane, even helicopter transportation, and entertaining them grandly with huge banquets lasting for hours! One teacher was taken one evening to the racetrack by a group of students. They went to the restaurant there, dislodged some people who were sitting at the best tables, proceeded to enjoy a festive dinner specially cooked for them and only for them.

One of the students had a groom bring one of his father's thoroughbred racehorses, and offered the teacher a ride. "Imagine, a race horse!" she exclaimed, marveling. "Here in the States no one, but no one except the jockey is ever allowed to ride such expensive animals!"

Another time they were whisked by helicopter to a luxurious lodge in the mountains for a boisterous party with men and women sporting gold jewelry and precious stones. "This had to be the Georgian mafia," they recounted. "We have never seen such a display of riches!"

As for me, in my double capacity as American and son of Noé Jordania, everywhere I went I was greeted and treated magnificently by ordinary Georgians as well as by the wealthy. I'll never forget how I walked into a bar on the beach with a friend just to see what it was like, as we had no money in our swimming suits. The bartender and his wife recognized me—I had been on TV several times — and we had to accept drinks and a bottle of cognac.

Another time three of us went to a restaurant in Borjomi, a celebrated Georgian spa. It was supposedly the best in town, but certainly did not look like much. Anyhow, we were first told that there was no food. Then our driver told the owners who I was, and lo and behold! Not only was a sumptuous dinner served, but they refused any payment and insisted we take with us several bottles of wine.

**Friday 6 September**

That August the United States Congress started paying attention to Georgia. The first-ever American to come to Tbilisi in his official capacity was Dana Rohrabacher, congressman from California. Three weeks later a congressional delegation arrived in a U.S. Government plane. Its mission was twofold: establish contact with President Gamsakhurdia and his government, and at the same time meet with leaders of the opposition and investigate allegations of human rights violations.

There were at that time a certain number of prisoners whom the Government called criminals, but everyone else considered political. Most prominent was a certain Jaba Ioseliani, leader of the Mkhedroni, a para-military organization which I am told interposed itself between Georgians and Ossetians during the troubles in Ossetia, and succeeded in averting bloodshed and protecting villages and property. This group was strongly anti-Gamsakhurdia, who had many of them arrested. They were accused of being terrorists who had assaulted various police and military installations and stolen weapons for their own use, and also of having blackmailed officials and wealthy people to obtain money to finance their activities.

The U.S. delegation remained in Georgia for about a week, and it is its arrival that indirectly led to the confrontations and armed clashes between opponents and government forces that were so widely reported in the West during September 1991.

Like Paris, Tbilisi is empty in August. People here have five weeks of official vacation per year, like most Europeans, and everybody goes to the country, mountains, or seaside. The Soviet economy may be in shambles, but it seems that every Georgian either has a dacha out of town or relatives in the country. And many traditionally go spend the month in a spa for the waters, like in Europe. The first day of September marks the return to work and the tempo of life picks up very noticeably.

The concurrence of the return from summer vacations and the presence of the American congressional delegation prompted the opposition leaders to call for a mass meeting the evening of Monday 2 September, 1991. The meeting took place in front of the Cinema House, under the statue of Shota Rustaveli, the great Georgian medieval poet. Several thousand peaceful participants attended. It ended tragically.

Even Zviad Gamsakhurdia's most ardent supporters could not understand why he sent his militia's riot squad to disperse the gathering. "If he had left them alone, they would have made speeches, then gone home," everybody said. But no, that would have been too sensible.

One hour into the meeting the riot police suddenly attacked using bludgeons and fire-arms. The ferocity of the assault took the participants by surprise, and in the melee that followed at least 60 were wounded, some seriously, and many more sustained bruises and minor injuries. Afterwards, Gamsakhurdia claimed he had never authorized the use of fire arms, that he only ordered the meeting to be suppressed because it had convened despite his express ban against demonstrations: "It was not the time to show disunity, with the American Congressional delegation in Tbilisi", he declared to explain his actions.

Those of us who were not at the meeting learned about the event not through the Georgian media, which is under tight government control, but by hearsay and then through the Russian news program. It seems that several amateurs video-taped the scene, and these documents were promptly send to the Russian and international media. We thus were able to see with our own eyes the brutality of the repression. Many people compared it to April 9, and even claimed it was much worse, because then, it was Russians soldiers against Georgian civilians, and now, it is Georgians against Georgians. Fortunately no one was killed. But everybody was deeply shocked by the incident, which triggered open clashes and demonstrations.

Barricades were raised on Rustaveli, the main thoroughfare; General Kitovani and his faction of the national guard joined the opposition; and agitation against Gamsakhurdia gathered momentum, fueled in part by the international community's condemnation of the government actions and policies, and reinforced by two former ministers who joined the ranks of the opposition: just before the Russian coup, the Georgian Prime Minister, Tengiz Sigua, and the Foreign Minister, Giorgi Khoshtaria, resigned because of deep disagreements with President Gamsakhurdia's authoritarian methods, heavy-handed internal policies, and inept handling of relations with Western countries, which at the same time he professed to court to enlist their help in the struggle for Georgian independence.

It is rather remarkable how the powers that be do not understand that armed repression is most often counterproductive, to say the least. In the Baltic States, for instance, violent repression led to a reinforcement of nationalism, eventually leading to full sovereignty. In Georgia, the April 9 tragedy firmed every Georgian's resolve to wrestle independence from the Soviets; and Gamsakhurdia's bloody repression of the September 2 meeting led to open revolt against his personal style of presidency and calls for his resignation a mere four months after he was elected president with close to 84% of the votes!

I absented myself from Tbilisi during a good part of September, traveling through Georgia and going hunting in the mountains of Daghestan.

Away from the capital, everything was calm, there

were no demonstrations, no clashes. Support for government or opposition varied from region to region. In Mingrelia, Gamsakhurdia's home province, almost everyone was for him. In Batumi, the opposition was dominant. Elsewhere, people were concerned with their immediate problems.

In the wine-growing province of Kakheti, everyone was preoccupied with the harvest. In Vardzia, the CAVE city near the Turkish border, the residents were concerned about the question of the possible return of the Meskhetian Turks, who had been expelled in 1944 by Stalin: "The only good thing Stalin ever did" was the general consensus. In Ossetia, strife continued, the Soviet army intervention being considered by the Georgians as helping the Ossetians, by the Ossetians as helping to preserve peace.

By and large, I would say, the villages and small towns were for Gamsakhurdia, while opposition to his heavy-handed rule was centered in the big cities, and mostly among the intellectuals and professional classes, who seemed more alert to his mistakes and short-sighted policies.

When I returned to Tbilisi later in the month, the situation seemed stabilized with the barricades still in place— there were only two— supposedly protecting the opposition headquarters on Rustaveli Avenue, located some 500 meters from Government House. There seemed to be permanent meetings in progress, both pro-Gamsakhurdia and against. Thousands of people milled about, strolling from one side to the other. But this was the calm before the tempest. Soon matters took a turn for the worse.

### Sunday 22 September

Big meeting in front of government house in support of Gamsakhurdia. Since last night he has been broadcasting appeals to the population on government radio and TV: "Three thousand bandits of the opposition armed with guns and pistols are setting siege to Government House. Come defend your Parliament and your President!" His cry for help elicited a tremendous response in the villages, particularly in Zviad's family's native province of Mingrelia.

Here is what happened in the village of Gali, according to an eyewitness: "Saturday around 10 p.m. the bells rang out and the sirens sounded the alarm. Everyone rushed to town hall believing that a fire or another catastrophe had happened. But the alarms were in response to Gamsakhurdia's hysterical appeal. Men grabbed their guns—everybody's armed in Georgia— women prepared supplies, buses and cars were assembled; and by the hundreds they careened off toward Tbilisi, seven hours away, to defend their President. But against whom?

I myself was in Tbilisi that Saturday evening, right in front of Government House. There was no sign of any attack or any siege. Members of the opposition, unarmed, were gathered a few hundred meters away, as they had been for the past three weeks. Soon we were to understand the reason for this call to arms. Under the smoke screen of a spurious uprising, in the wee hours of the morning at about 4 a.m., "volunteers" supporting the government destroyed the two pitiful barricades that had been erected by members of the opposition. These commandos invaded the general headquarters of the two main opposition parties, which had been established on Rustaveli Avenue for quite a long time, at least a year. There they bodily threw out the opposition members and destroyed or stole documents.

I was told that there were a large number of casualties and that tear gas was used. The government however issued a statement claiming that the militia took no part in this action, while other sources claimed that the police had arrested some 30 opposition members. As a media blackout is in effect — even the usual news broadcasts from Moscow have been cut— we do not know what to believe. As for the newspapers, only those that are pro-government are authorized; the Russian papers are no longer available.

**Monday 23 September**
Rustaveli Avenue is now blocked to any kind of vehicle not by barricades, but with trucks and buses. People can walk along freely, however, and many take advantage of the situation to stroll in the street itself, now free from circulation. In fact it is very pleasant like this without the cars and their leaded exhaust fumes. I hope that when the situation goes back to normal the authorities will get the idea, and close the avenue to car traffic on weekends and perhaps also some evenings, as it is done in some cities in other parts of the world.

With all these crowds there is not a single street vendor. Imagine this in Paris or New York: they would be here in force, trying to make a buck. It would probably be the same in Armenia: in Yerevan, even in normal times, there are many street vendors, while in Tbilisi there are practically none.

Like the Moscow metro, the metro in Tbilisi is deep underground. It is entered by long steep escalators, since it was dug way below the hills of the city and crosses under the Mtkvari River several times. As in Moscow, every station has three sets of escalators—one going up and one going down, with the third kept in reserve or in a state of repair (or disrepair, as the case may be). For the first time today, at the metro stop "Freedom", the stop closest to Government House, there were two up escalators in use instead of the usual one— clearly in expectation of the crowds coming to the help of the President. Also for the first time, there were militia on duty on the metro platforms. But all these precautions were for nothing: not many came and there was no disorder.

Poor Zviad! He seems to have no understanding of the niceties of foreign policy. He calls for Western countries to recognize the independence of Georgia, and at the same time insults those who could help him, including President Bush and Secretary of State Baker, whom he calls "unwitting dupes of the Kremlin". But is there still a Kremlin, in the old meaning of the name?

The president's supporters seem to be more numerous than the opposition's, but appearances are misleading. One has only to see the hundreds of government-leased buses stationed on Rustaveli Avenue and nearby streets, which came from all the corners of Georgia. They are here because Zviad ordered each of his prefects to send a minimum of 100 supporters to Tbilisi - this alone brings the total to at least 4,000 people. Only one prefect, I am told, refused to comply. He was immediately dismissed.

These "spontaneous" demonstrators have already been here for two weeks, of course at the expense of the government. The opposition, in contrast, does not have the material means to be able to "import" its supporters. The members of the opposition who are assembled on Rustaveli Avenue are for the most part from Tbilisi.

Great progress on Georgian TV: it now broadcasts intermittently, at most two hours a day; but that's a lot better than just after the September 2 incident, when from morning to night it was ramming Zviad down our throats: Zviad making speeches; Zviad leading the mourning ceremonies in honor of Merab Kostava [a Georgian nationalist killed in an auto accident in 1989]; Zviad opening Parliament; Zviad kissing children and shaking hands; Zviad greeting the international delegations at the European Water-Ski Competition in Poti last July; Zviad's supporters shouting his praise, particularly older women shaking their bodies in ecstasy, while invoking his name as though he were the announced Messiah. It was rather unsettling, reminiscent of the cult of personality, as Khrushchev used to say. And to think that in Stalin's time the whole Soviet Union was behaving that way!

Does President Gamsakhurdia really understand nothing in international politics? Or has he deliberately chosen to antagonize Western countries and the USSR so that he can depict Georgia as under attack and thus strengthen his popularity among certain layers of society and thus consolidate his power? It seems very possible, since he finds his supporters mainly amongst Georgian ideologues similar to the America Firsters and other chauvinist groups. Hence his insistence on Georgia for the Georgians, on the integrity of the Georgian territory (including Abkhazia and the so-called South Ossetia), on traditional Georgian customs and civilization, on the Georgian rite of orthodox Christianity, in short on the narrowest concept of Georgia. Of course, one underlying reason for his success is that the Georgians are keenly aware that their country has been in practice a Russian colony for most of the past two centuries. The desire to escape this colonial status is very powerful.

Most Russians totally fail to understand the aspirations to freedom of the outlying republics, particularly Georgia. They say: "We have lived together for two centuries. We never had any trouble. We Russians shed our blood for the Georgians when we came to help them against the Persians and the Turks. So why this sudden desire for separation? Why this enmity?"

Yes, even my good Russian friend Tatiana, who is otherwise so enlightened, speaks in those terms. "We entered freely in an association of our two countries two centuries ago," she mistakenly asserts. "Georgian nobles were favored by the tsar even over Russian nobles," she continues truly enough. "So why this anti-Russian sentiment of all Georgians, at this late date?"

The eternal complaint of the colonizer against the ingratitude of the colonized. We heard that from the French in

Algeria, the British in India, the Dutch in Indonesia....
And Tatiana conveniently forgets the invasion of Free
Georgia by the Red army in 1921, advancing from North,
South, and East a scant few months after a solemn treaty of
non-aggression had been signed in Moscow between Russia
and Georgia — the first of a long list of treaties broken by the
communists whenever it suited their designs. Nevertheless, I
have not encountered a significant anti-Russian people
sentiment in Georgia, but rather a firm anti-Russian hegemony
resolve.

"They are all out of their mind, these Moldavians,
Estonians, Georgians, Armenians. Don't they see that we are
in it together, that we need each other?" continues Tatiana,
totally oblivious to reality. She doesn't know, or does not want
to know that Moldavia is in fact largely Romanian, that the
Baltic States were incorporated forcibly in the Soviet Union
during WWII, that the same happened to Georgia in 1921, that
even Ukraine has been denied its own identity for centuries,
and so on.... None of those countries are Russia, and while it
may well be that they will have to remain within the Soviet
economic sphere for some time to come, freedom for them
means the political freedom to assert their own national and
linguistic identity, to be able to decide each for themselves
their own destiny. Will this really come to pass?

Coming back to Georgia: Zviad, having managed to
identify himself in the eyes of many with the very idea of
independence, considers all those who oppose him as traitors,
— traitors to Georgia, traitors to independence, enemies of the
people. They all are "agents of the Kremlin", including Sigua
and Khoshtaria, who until a month ago were Gamsakhurdia's
own Prime Minister and Foreign Affairs Minister. Zviad
labels his domestic opponents "allies and accomplices of this
group of Georgians who live in exile in Moscow and are led by
the sculptor Tsereteli and by Eduard Shevardnadze" —a man

Zviad must be terribly afraid of, since he attacks him so vehemently and so often. And all those who hold Shevardnadze in esteem are also under suspicion, including President Bush, Secretary of State Baker, France's President Mitterand, German Chancellor Kohl, and many others.

**Thursday 26 September**

Here are some unconfirmed details of what happened on September 21, that Saturday night and Sunday morning when the so-called "storm troopers" arrived. Late in the evening, a group of women climbed the main barricade on Rustaveli Avenue, microphone in hand, accused the opposition of being traitors to Georgia, "unworthy of drinking its pure waters," and offered them a quite different drink. Allegedly, these women lifted their skirts and pissed in public on the barricades! Such an obscene act is totally unthinkable in Georgia, and I don't remember such an incident in any country before.

I heard later that these women were common criminals who were brought from the prison and promised shortened sentences or immediate freedom, if they acted that way. This I quite believe: ordinary Georgian women are so very reserved, their demeanor so modest that it would be hard to imagine them willingly acting that way, even under the influence of political hysteria.

Then around 4 o'clock in the morning, a well-disciplined troop of some 300 men suddenly attacked. This attack was described as savage, and in fact 68 people are still in the hospital at this writing, 48 hours later, some seriously wounded, some still suffering the consequences of tear gas. The aggressors demolished the barricades with the help of the heavy equipment they brought with them. They invaded the headquarters of the two main opposition groups, where they had been installed for over a year. This is why Rustaveli Avenue is now calm. The opposition has been expelled and only supporters of Gamsakhurdia remain.

The president claims that neither militia nor national guardsmen were involved in this brutal assault. Witnesses, however, conclude that considering the discipline and organization of the action it is difficult to believe the attackers were only volunteers. Many believe that it was a military or paramilitary force in plainclothes.

Some official sources say that during the fight inside the general headquarters of the opposition, a young man, Irakli Tsereteli, was pushed or fell from a high widow and was killed. Another man was said to have sacrificed himself by dousing himself with gasoline and setting himself on fire. (NB: This last incident was confirmed, but the government's position is that the opposition instigated his burning himself.)

**Sunday 29 September**

Last night there was shooting around the TV building. It seems that some of the government forces consisting of shock troops of the militia, also known as OMO, with some trainees, attacked the opponents' positions. They were repulsed and two OMOs were killed. A busload of those trainees was also captured, but they were set free.

Thursday night government forces recaptured Shavnabada, the military camp that was held by General Kitovani and his rebel national guardsmen. Government television announced that the camp was recaptured without any casualties, after a resistance that lasted just about 15 minutes, as Kitovani and most of his people had already left. However I was told by opposition members that there were at least five dead, and that the BBC mentioned there were some 60 casualties. We continue to be in the dark, since all TV and radio news are strictly controlled by the government. There is no Russian TV, no Russian or foreign newspapers.

Heard yesterday that the U.S. and Finland are offering asylum to Georgian political refugees, and also that Germany

212

and other European countries declared that no help whatsoever will go to Georgia as long as Gamsakhurdia is in power, but that if he resigns they'll provide all kinds of aid. That sounds, to me, like wishful thinking.

**Monday 30 September**
It looks like the president has won, at least for the moment. The opposition doesn't seem to realize it yet, but it became clear to me already a few days ago, when government forces managed to extend their protected perimeter by blocking streets much farther from government house; and even more telling, when he issued the order that all liquor shops be closed, everyone obeyed. Now what remains against him is an increasingly isolated group of demonstrators clustered around Television House. They control the building, but do not control the airwaves, nor do they control any of the means of communication.

What a mistake, not to have seized them from the beginning! They do control a few armored troop carriers, a couple of heavy guns, and several heavy-duty machine guns, which they positioned so as to avoid a repetition of the September 24 night attack on their former headquarters; but I think it will be of no avail. A friend tells me they have powerful mortars aimed at Government House and the TV tower dominating the city, but that means nothing: whoever uses heavy weapons will most certainly loose.

Yes, it certainly looks like President Gamsakhurdia and his entourage are going to stay in power, pushing for and enforcing their authoritarian policies and antagonizing the whole world. Well, the Georgians will have the government they voted for.

I feel sorry for the opponents, among which I count many friends, and for all those who do not deserve such a leadership. But very clearly, a large majority is for Zviad and his narrowly nationalistic program. Never mind that under

213

another name he is perpetuating the communist system of government — read system of bribes and influence peddling.

The new regime kept intact all the communist structures, simply replacing the people in charge with its own loyalists, who are busily filling their pockets, just like the communists before them used to do; with the difference that bribery became worse than ever. The communists were fairly moderate in their demands for baksheesh, since they were in their positions for the long run. But the new people do not know how long they will last, and therefore are in a hurry to get rich.

**Wednesday 2 October**

Yesterday Hamlet came to see me. Yes, quite a few Georgians sport a first name taken from English literature: Hamlet is a favorite, but I have also met Desdemonas, Otellos, Gullivers, Ophelias....

This Hamlet is a young man very active in the opposition, standing guard with a rifle all night, participating in all debates, discussions. I gave him some dollars, which he accepted only after long protests, and only when it occurred to me to tell him that he should consider this money as a loan. I explained that he might soon need some foreign currency, as he and his friends may well have to slip over the border into Turkey, since the government was sure to retaliate as soon as it rallies its forces.

He asked me what I thought about going into the mountains and waging guerilla warfare. In my opinion, I told him, such an action would be totally unproductive and self-defeating, primarily because it is precisely in the remote villages and towns that Zviad has his most fervent supporters. The guerrillas would find no help among the population, quite the contrary: the villagers themselves would hunt them. And then, if the guerrillas would kill anyone, they would be condemned by all.

It looks like many opponents will have to flee the country. Fortunately Georgia is still officially part of the Soviet Union, and the Georgians can freely go live anywhere in any of the republics, without need of visa, asylum, or anything. I do hope they'll leave in time, since the Zviadists may well exact revenge, loudly applauded by their supporters. As for justice being impartial, forget it. Seventy years of communism, following 120 years of tsarism, following 2000 years of feudalism, have taught judges but one thing: obey the powers that be!

The democratic opposition is thinking about plans for the future, since it is clear Gamsakhurdia has the upper hand right now. I again advised them to prepare a line of retreat: clothes, money, i.d. papers somewhere away from home or known relatives' or friend's home, in a place where they could hide a few days and then leave for other parts of the USSR. And after that, work on the political angle.

Some hotheads asked me what I thought about a Zviad assassination. I strongly advised against even contemplating such an act: first of all, this is no way to build democracy. And then any attempt would be sure to reinforce the Zviadists, and, if successful, would make a martyr of Zviad and completely discredit the opposition. Someone would take his place, and the situation would become even more polarized with the full support of an outraged populace.

**Thursday 4 October**

The number of otherwise intelligent people who believe Zviad and his propaganda never ceases to astound me. Yet any kind of reflection shows that belief has nothing to do with intelligence, and that throughout the ages many intelligent people believed the most outrageous propaganda: witness wars of religion, Stalinism, Reverend Jones, fascism, and so many other -isms.

Last night a conductor/composer of my acquaintance

came to see me. He wanted me to mail a letter in the U.S. He is an affable man of perhaps 40 years of age, highly educated, articulate, intelligent. Yet, as we were talking about the once-again postponement of the beginning of school in Tbilisi, he said in all seriousness, referring to the opponents, and more specifically to the head of the rebel national guard faction: "They are bandits. That's why school is postponed. This Kitovani would think nothing of kidnapping a classroom of children and holding them hostage!" It must be the same type of people who strongly believe that "these Ossetians tore Georgian children in two," or that "the Meskhetians used to torture horribly Georgian men and women."

This trend is the more worrisome that traditionally in Georgia there has not been any significant ethnic strife. There has never been any pogrom, and Georgians highly respect and like Israel, with which country they have many links. In fact, while all air-links to the outside world have to go through Moscow or Leningrad, no matter which part of the USSR one comes from, there is one exception: a direct air link between Tbilisi and Tel-Aviv!

Also, I remember that during World War II, when the Germans were occupying Paris, my father and his associates wrote for the German authorities a brief to the effect that Georgian Jews were not racially Jewish, but were ethnic Georgians who had adopted the Jewish religion way back in the Middle-Ages. As a result, the Georgian Jews living in Nazi-dominated Europe were never molested.

Despite the existence of disputed territories, there has not been any clash with the neighboring Azerbaijan or Armenia —except for a short flare-up in 1918. Kurds living here declare themselves perfectly free to do as they wish: there are some 60,000 Kurds in Tbilisi, 200,000 in Georgia. Leks, Ingush, Chechens, Avars—all Moslems— come and go freely, and many live here. So do many Russians, Armenians, Turks,

Greeks, and even, I am told, since the '50's a few American black families. Until recently Abkhazians and Ossetians lived here peacefully, with their own schools and even a college in the Ossetian language.

This does not mean that there were no fights. Of course there were, and wars, and invasions throughout the centuries; but they were not particularly ethnic in nature. For instance, the mountain people would traditionally swoop down on the Georgian villages and capture and take away what they could. Retaliation would of course follow. But this was tribal, territorial, even ritual, not ethnic. And while Georgians served in the tsarist armies to help put down the Daghestanian Shamil's long rebellion, he still became a hero not only among his countrymen, but in Georgia as well.

That makes the present trend even more ominous. Tales of atrocities are always used to whip up nationalistic fervor and can easily lead to real atrocities. We have seen this all too often, alas.

Whether they are for or against Gamsakhurdia, whether they are monarchists, democrats, social-democrats, or of fascist tendencies, whatever their gender, age, or social status, most Georgians agree on two basic things: Georgia must be independent, and South Ossetia and Abkhazia must remain an integral part of Georgia. Personally I think the Georgians' claim about so-called South Ossetia is valid. Their claim against Abkhazia is less convincing.

South Ossetia, an area the size of Rhode Island, was always called Inner Kartli. It was only in 1922, in order to weaken Georgia, and in order to reward Ossetians who helped put down a Georgian rebellion, that it was administratively separated from Georgia and given its present name. The OssetIANS are a Christian tribe, linguistically related to the Iranians. Ossetia proper is located on the other side of the Caucasian divide.

It is only since the 18th century — a drop in the bucket given Georgia's 3000 years history — that Ossetians have been living in the Inner Kartli area. In the provincial capital, Tskhinvali, there were in the 1920's only four to nine Ossetian families versus many more Georgian households. Ossetians and Georgians lived peacefully side-by-side, the former having their own schools and even a college in the Ossetian language. Note that there is no college in their own land, Northern Ossetia!

Communications between Northern and Southern Ossetia were very poor, since the mountain passes were closed by inclement weather most of the year. It is only recently that the Roki tunnel was dug, so that communications improved, and more Ossetians came to live in the South where conditions are better. Thus it is clear that for the Georgians to claim that province means reinstating the borders from before 1922.

As for Abkhazia: Abkhazians constitute about 20% of the population, versus at least 45% Georgians, the rest comprising many other ethnicities. But Abkhazia was always Abkhazia, the Georgians do not deny it. They claim though that it was always part of Georgia, like the other provinces such as Mingrelia, Guria and Kakheti, and should remain so even more because so many Georgians live there.

Personally I am not yet totally convinced. However, there are even less compelling arguments for Abkhazia to become part of Russia: the only reason why some—not all—Abkhazians want this is in order to retain their privileged position: most government posts are theirs, and the number of deputies is almost evenly divided between Georgians and Abkhazians, the latter having two more. So that in effect the Abkhazians elect at least three times more deputies than the Georgians, relative to population.

An amusing note: when the Georgian president Gamsakhurdia met the president of Abkhazia recently, he spoke in Abkhazian, but the Abkhazian president spoke in Russian because he does not know his own language! I hope we shall soon see these conflicts resolved, now that it is no longer in the-all-but-defunct Communist party's power to foment strife. And then the South Ossetians and the Abkhazians leaders managed to discredit themselves in the eyes of all by siding with the hard-line communist junta on August 19.

I fervently hope Georgia, Abkhazia, and the new Russian Republic will know how to collaborate to impartially handle the problem.

**Friday 5 October**

I am leaving tomorrow for Moscow, and am looking forward to watching the news and reading Pravda and Izvestia.

What irony! Only 6 weeks ago the Russian media was hard-line communist, not to be trusted, and now it is truly informative. The August 19 coup led to a real liberation of Russia, but here in Tbilisi we are more and more restricted. Our main source of information is hearsay: the Georgian newspapers, radio and television are strictly government controlled, and there is still no Russian TV broadcasts, nor any Russian or foreign periodicals.

Few Western broadcasts deal any longer with Georgia. It is always sobering to listen to foreign news. We think that Tbilisi should be at the center of attention, or at least worth a few words: far from it! Now that there is hardly any active violence here, most of the time Georgia is not even mentioned, even though it was big news earlier in September.

When I arrive in the States, I intend to peruse American and European back issues of magazines and newspapers. It will be most interesting to compare the journalistic accounts of the Moscow coup and the Tbilisi disorders to my own direct perception of these same events.

I well remember how surprised I was many years ago when I read written accounts of the Liberation of Paris in August 1944. I had been then living in Paris, and had been an eye-witness, wandering all over town to see as much as I possibly could. Yet the later accounts differed markedly from my recollections, and seemed to me extraordinarily romanticized and glamorized. I wonder if the same will come to pass with this summer's exciting happenings in what will soon be the former Soviet Union.

———————————

# Aftermath

The demonstrations against the regime continued sporadically throughout the fall. In late December 1991, following yet another brutal attempt to repress a demonstration near Parliament, the National Guard and the paramilitary group *Mkhedrioni* (horsemen) initiated a military action that caused considerable damage in the center of town and resulted in the overthrow of Gamsakhurdia, who fled Tbilisi 6 January 1992. That was just about one week after the official dissolution of the Soviet Union, which took place the 31st December 1991 at midnight.

There followed a long period of instability and civil war. When the situation stabilized in 1995 with the election of Edward Shevardnadze as president of Georgia, we resumed our Summer English Language Institute, ending the program several years later when official institutions took over our self-imposed task.

## A quick historical look (from Wikipedia)

After Gamsakhurdia's overthrow, the country became embroiled in a bitter civil war which lasted almost until 1995. Eduard Shevardnadze returned to Georgia in 1992 and joined the leaders of the coup – Kitovani and Ioseliani – to head a triumvirate called the "State Council".

In 1995, Shevardnadze was officially elected as president of Georgia. At the same time, simmering disputes within two regions of Georgia, Abkhazia and South Ossetia, between local separatists and the majority Georgian populations, erupted into widespread inter-ethnic violence and wars. Supported by Russia, Abkhazia and South Ossetia, with the exception of some "pockets" of territory, achieved de facto independence from Georgia. Roughly 230,000 to 250,000 Georgians were expelled from Abkhazia by Abkhaz separatists and North Caucasians volunteers (including Chechens) in 1992–1993. Around 23,000 Georgians fled South Ossetia as well, and many

## Aftermath

Ossetian families were forced to abandon their homes in the Borjomi region and moved to Russia.

In 2003, Shevardnadze (who won reelection in 2000) was deposed by the Rose Revolution, after Georgian opposition and international monitors asserted that the November 2 parliamentary elections were marred by fraud. The revolution was led by Mikheil Saakashvili, Zurab Zhvania and Nino Burjanadze, former members and leaders of Shevardnadze's ruling party. Mikheil Saakashvili was elected as President of Georgia in 2004 and re-elected in 2008 for a 5-year term.

---

# AFTERWORD: Leuville 2011

**The Village**

The village center has not changed since my youth. The long main street is lined with the same low houses that have been refurbished and somewhat modernized over the years. They are no longer small farms but merely dwellings: produce cultivation was abandoned long ago. But the bakery is still there at the end of the street and so is the hotel restaurant on the central square opposite the iron gate of the chateau, as well as the deli near the postern just after the abrupt jog in the street that was always considered a place for an accident to happen. The village remains very quiet: there is little movement, especially now that the busses no longer stop in the square. The only real traffic happens in the evening when people return from work by car. Leuville has basically become a dormitory town.

The small surrounding fields have all but disappeared. In their place are a bunch of small houses surrounded by small gardens. There are almost no building lots left. The chateau stands as the largest property in the region, with its lawns, gardens and fields open to the heavens. It goes without saying that it is lusted after by many powers that be, mainly developers.

**The Chateau**

The physical appearance of the property has hardly changed. The surrounding stonewall is still moss-eaten, the big iron gate is still painted green, the postern is still encased in the wall. The great avenue of lime trees is still there, and so are the big trees at the back of the domain, with the difference that some have succumbed to the ravages of weather and time.

The chateau itself also has remained almost unchanged—but this was accomplished with great effort, for the maintenance of such a large building requires a lot of money and energy. Shortly after the war the vast roof threatened to collapse, which would have brought about an inexorable deterioration. But fortunately my mother, with her indomitable energy, succeeded in obtaining considerable subsidies from a Swedish charity, allowing much needed repairs that were so well made they have lasted until today. A few years ago, a windstorm removed a portion of the slate roof, but since the repairs of nearly a half-century ago were made carefully, the slate could be replaced without too much damage, although the work took months. Other important maintenance was done, such as drying the basement and repairing a load-bearing wall that threatened to collapse because of insidious water infiltrations, which caused a lot of damage before they were discovered.

Over the years most room and ancillary buildings have been upgraded: there is now running water everywhere, and the occupants have installed toilets, bathrooms and individual heating. To date seven families are housed year-round in the chateau and outbuildings. Many other Georgians use their rooms only on summer weekends to escape the heat of the big city, which is just a 30-minute drive away. Others still spend the whole warm season, like my sister Nathela, who loves it there.

Generally the chateau is very quiet, except when the Georgians gather for a formal occasion, as happens quite often: a national holiday, funeral, wedding, christening, birthday or fair open to the whole village. The events take place outdoors on the lawn, a few hundred people sitting around long tables in the Georgian manner, or if the weather turns bad, in the central hall, which has hardly changed since the time of my childhood: a large room where over a hundred guests can be seated, its wall covered with mementoes and portraits of the time of the Georgian Republic of 1918-1921, with the portrait of my father at the place of honor, surrounded by portraits of his associates.

Now that Georgia has stabilized as an independent democratic country, the time has come to fulfill the wish of my father and his associates and to devolve the domain to Georgia. This transfer involves rather intricate legal procedures which might take time, but the principle has been established wherewith the Chateau is to become a Franco-Georgian cultural center where the memories of the First Republic and its government in exile will be forever preserved.

**The Cemetery**

Since my childhood the Georgian part of the village cemetery has been greatly expanded to accommodate successive generations. French law generally reserves cemeteries for the local town people, but notwithstanding the general rule, non-resident Georgians may be buried in Leuville through a special dispensation, mainly because the Georgian colony funded the successive extensions of the cemetery and the stone wall that surrounds it, and takes monetary charge of its maintenance.

Our cemetery remains the common center for all Georgians, not only those living in France but those living abroad, as well. Many who came to the end of their lives in the United States, South America, and other distant countries chose to be buried there.

The number of descendants of the original Georgian exiles keeps increasing, and so is the number of new immigrants. Thus it can be expected that our Leuville cemetery will always be part of the Georgian collective consciousness and will remain a place of pilgrimage for our people, wherever they actually live. Indeed Georgians from Georgia who come to France make it their honor and duty to visit the cemetery and pay their respects to the patriots who repose there, especially to my father.

His grave is at the place of honor in the cemetery. On his tombstone are inscribed these words in Georgian and French:

> *Noé Jordania, 1868-1953, first President of the Georgian Republic, to whom Georgia owes its having recovered national sovereignty on 26 May 1918, after 117 years of Russian domination.*

In the same vault are buried my mother Ina Koreneva, my sister Asmath and her husband Levan Pagava. Some day not too distant we shall join them, my sister Nathela and I.

*********************

*Leuville 2011*

# POSTSCRIPT
## Reflections on my Georgias

During the 20 years since Georgia regained its independence in 1991, its successive governments have shown a strangely neglectful, if not downright negative attitude towards the First Georgian Republic of 1918-1921 and the selfless men and women who created it from the ruins of the tsarist empire.

In 2009, at the occasion of the 90th anniversary of the Georgian Declaration of Independence of 26 May 1918, I participated in Tbilisi in a conference on *The Birth of Modern Georgia* that attempted among other topics to address this neglect.

After the conference I was asked to write a preface to the ensuing publication. I am reprinting it here for those interested in this facet of Georgia's modern history.

\*\*\*\*\*\*\*\*\*\*\*\*\*\*\*

## THE BIRTH OF MODERN GEORGIA:
### THE FIRST REPUBLIC AND ITS SUCCESSORS, 1918-2009

### A Preface
### *Redjeb Jordania*

My very first visit to Georgia was in 1990. In the fall of that year my niece Ethery Pagava and her Paris-based ballet company, together with her husband the well-known French folk singer Jacques Douai, were invited for a tour in Moscow, Tbilisi, Kutaisi and Yerevan, and they asked me to join them as a pianist. It had been a very long time since I had played the piano professionally, but despite my misgivings I could not miss such a long-awaited occasion.

The show was an enormous success, particularly in Georgia where the presence on stage of Noé Jordania's son and his grand-daughter did not fail to attract even more attention. After the tour was over I came back from Yerevan to Tbilisi, where I stayed a few months to get to know better the country of my ancestors and to witness the exciting and chaotic events of the period. Thus it happened that one afternoon, as I was sitting in a café in Tbilisi with a couple of Georgian friends, some people at an adjoining table asked: "Who is that man? Is he an American, or what?"

My friend answered: "Yes, he comes from America, but he is really a Georgian: he is the son of our First president, Noé Jordania."

They could not, would not believe it despite my friends' assurances. "If he really were the son of Noé Jordania, there would be a huge to-do here, he would not be sitting in a café just like that."

Well, there was no huge to-do. In fact, there was no "to-do" at all. And now in the year 2009, almost 20 years after the regained independence, there is still no "huge to-do". There is no official recognition of our First republic, no real acknowledgement of the many thousands of Georgians who sacrificed their lives for an independent Georgian state, and to whom Georgia is indebted for having recovered its unity and independence after 115 years of Tsarist occupation, seven centuries of internal disarray, and subjection to external powers; there is even no real recognition of the simple fact that present-day Georgia in many ways draws on the legacy and achievements of the Georgian republic of 1918-1921, of which it is a continuation after a 70-year hiatus – somewhat like the French Republic was restored in 1871 after some 70 years of royalty and empire.

I was present Thursday 15 November 1990 when the First freely-elected parliament in more that seventy years convened in Tbilisi. At that memorable session Zviad Gamsakhurdia was elected President of Parliament, and, in an enormously emotional moment, the Soviet era flags were lowered from all public places and replaced with the red, black and white flag of the First republic. At that same session the date of May 26, the day my father Noé Jordania declared independence in 1918, was proclaimed Independence Day.

Yet during those magnificent and exciting days, as well as during Zviad Gamsakhurdia's short-lived presidency, there was practically no mention of the First Republic. Under his successor Eduard Shevardnadze there were some minor gestures to the republic's memory. As the son of Noé Jordania, I was given the title *Honorary Citizen of Georgia*. A small display of important documents from the First Republic and a "Hall of the First Republic" were established inside the parliament building, which, significantly, was not open to the public. That's all.

In 2004 a new generation of Georgian revolutionaries led by Michael Saakashvili took power. They were young, idealistic, ambitious, and energetic. But in sweeping away the old Soviet-style regime, they also swept away the flag, coat of arms, and anthem of the First Republic.

For the young neophytes in power the Shevardnadze and Gamsakhurdia eras were their points of reference; they knew little about the 1918-1921 period or the 1924 insurrection when thousands of Georgian patriots, whether Social Democrats or National Democrats and Social Federalists, fought against newly established Soviet power.

The new Georgian leaders, most of whom were in their thirties, did not realize, perhaps, that for all of us in emigration, during 70 years of Soviet occupation, the three-colored Georgian flag symbolized our lost country. Yet they retained May 26 as Independence Day, thus implicitly admitting the importance of the First Republic.

President Saakashvili has slowly come to acknowledge Georgia's pre-Soviet experience of independent statehood. In his speeches, he refers at times to Noé Jordania, and he renamed an avenue on the Mtkvari River embankment after my father. He had previously named the road on the other side of the river for Zviad Gamsakhurdia, thus recognizing two presidents: Noé Jordania, who was the main actor in recreating a unified and free Georgia from the ruins of the tsarist empire; and Zviad Gamsakhurdia, whose presidency, cut short by an armed revolt, was followed by a civil war that cost thousands of victims, if not tens of thousands, as well as the loss Abakhazia and the so-called South Ossetia.

But why is it that successive independent Georgian governments have largely ignored the First Republic? Thinking about this over many years, I have come up with a number of hypotheses.

First, of course, is the issue of Soviet propaganda. Paradoxically, the greatest enemy of Soviet communism was socialism, since it competed for the allegiance of the same social classes. Indeed, as we know, the Georgian social-democrats, who were aligned with the ideas of European socialist parties, easily triumphed in post-tsarist Georgia. As soon as the Soviets took power after the 1921 invasion they imposed an unrelenting propaganda against the Democratic Republic of Georgia--if they mentioned it at all, which wasn't very often. This suppression and misrepresentation went on for close to 70 years!

Thus for three generations Georgians either knew nothing or very little about their first independent republic, and what they were told was sharply negative. Even if they mistrusted authority, those negative impressions had to remain embedded in the collective psyche, perhaps in a vague sort of way, but there nevertheless. *"Calomniez, calomniez, il en restera toujours quelque chose!"* as Beaumarchais famously wrote in « Le Barbier de Séville ». *(Slander, slander, some of it will always remain.)*

Along with this state induced amnesia, there was a Georgian fascination with the Middle Ages. In the mid-1980s, when the movement for independence was gathering strength, Georgians in search of their past turned toward a period of Georgian glory the Soviet state had allowed – even encouraged – them to remember: the era of the great Georgian kings in the 11th and 12th centuries.

When I first encountered Georgia in 1990, with so much excitement about Georgia's future in the air, I could not understand the fascination for such distant centuries: how was it, I asked myself, that people who claim to be interested in integrating into the modern world dwell on the 12th century?

Yet they did and still do, as evidenced by the present national flag, a combination of religious symbols revived from ancient times, which directly rejects the secular values of the First Republic.

This leads me to a third reason as to why the First Republic has lost its historical élan. To achieve independence from the tsarist empire, the First Republic had to break the notion of autocracy by divine right. This meant moving away from religion in order to diminish the tsar's grip on the popular mentality and join the modern world of secular republics.

The Georgia of today, by contrast, has broken away from the atheistic Soviet system. This has led to an opposite swing of the pendulum, this time toward Christianity, a direction which dovetailed nicely with the Georgians' medieval nostalgia. Thus the First Republic proclaimed separation of church and state, as is the case in the US and France among others, whereas contemporary Georgia has moved in a diametrically opposite direction, and proclaimed Georgian Orthodoxy the preferred national religion, with special privileges granted by the state in its 2002 Concordat with the church. Secularism and any form of socialism are constantly condemned by Orthodox leaders, who are among the most trusted individuals in the country.

This brings me naturally to my fourth point. The full name of the U.S.S.R. is the Union of Socialist Soviet Republics. It incorporates the dreaded word "socialist", which in the minds of soviet and post-soviet citizens is associated with the worst excesses of Stalinism. For most Georgians, socialism has become a dirty word, even though successful European models of social democracies are there for all to see.

Finally, there is the question of political and economic orientation. The Georgian Democratic Republic was the first social-democratic state in the world – quite remarkable given the region it occupied, its neighbors, and the times (civil war and revolution). But after the global crisis of World War One, new ways of thinking – such as social-democracy – became part of the movement for democratic and civil rights.

In contrast, after the 1990 independence Soviet attitudes and ways of thought persisted for a long time despite a proclaimed Western orientation, while today's Georgia is resolutely following the example of the free-market right-leaning American model. Thus Social-Democracy has been discredited as an alternative in the minds of Georgians, along with the Georgian Democratic Republic.

While there has been little official recognition of Noé Jordania, a great many people, even very young people, do know and respect his name. Whenever I find myself with a group of Georgians, be they delegates to a Diaspora convention or a group of students, many want to have their picture taken with me as a direct link to their very first democratic leader, Noé Jordania. Yet misconceptions and ignorance about the First Republic continue, among people in power as well as among Western experts. A case in point is former Assistant Deputy Secretary of State Ronald Asmus's account of the August 2008 war.

Entitled *The little war that shook the world* (Palgrave/McMillan, Jan. 2010), Asmus tries to explain the patriotic feelings that motivated President Saakashvili and the Georgians by going back to the First Republic of 1918-21. He writes: "The decision by the government in Tbilisi then (in 1921) not to fight for their independence left a legacy that would shape Saakashvili's decision in August 2008.

It had taken Georgia seventy years to regain its independence and many Georgians were not about to give it up a second time without a fight." And he repeats several times in his book the astonishing assertion that the 1921 Georgian government chose not to fight the invading Red Army.

Nothing could be further from the truth: in reality, in February 1921 the Red Army attacked with overwhelming numbers from Armenia, Azerbaijan, and from the north. Turkish troops, interested in seizing Georgia's Black Sea port of Batumi, invaded from the south. There was fierce resistance from the Georgian armed forces, and it took one full month for the Red Army to occupy all of little Georgia. A grace note: in a quixotic gesture, the remains of the Georgian army attacked and chased the Turks from Batumi and Adjaria before going themselves into exile.

I suspect that Asmus's erroneous belief comes from the Georgian government circles in which he moved, since where else could Mr.Asmus have learned it?

As this example shows once again, no country can afford to ignore part its history.

This is in part why we convened our conference. *The Birth of Modern Georgia* constitutes a step toward fulfilling a very important and practical need: to show Georgians and the world that democracy in Georgia, although late and imperfect by Western standards, has a century-old history; that the First Republic, although politically very different from the present regime, was nevertheless its progenitor; that the First Republic fought with all its might against the overwhelming strength of the Red Army invasion of 1921; that the Noé Jordania government never capitulated and went into exile to continue the struggle only after a vote of the Georgian Parliament ordered it to do so; and, finally, that Modern Georgia was born on 26 May 1918 when President Jordania declared independence from the Hall of Mirrors of what was then the Vorontsov Palace in Tbilisi.

Our conference was planned for May 2008 to mark the 90th anniversary of Georgian independence. However the turbulent events of the period forced successive postponements: demonstrations in Tbilisi in fall 2007; presidential elections in early 2008; parliamentary elections in May; and finally the August 2008 Russo-Georgian conflict.

When the conference finally took place in October 2009 it was a great success, bringing together international scholars and politicians whose interventions led to important parallels between the First Republic and Georgia's situation today. Also, it was instrumental in helping bring about positive results. At the beginning of 2010, the Hall of Mirrors, where the 1918 declaration of independence was announced, was renamed the Hall of the First Republic. A bust of my father is to be installed in the adjoining park, where I am sure my father strolled when considering important government decisions. Plans for a museum of the First Republic or a permanent exhibit in the national museum are going forward. It looks like after two decades, some recognition is in the works.

My father's grave remains in the Georgian cemetery of Leuville near Paris where he died in 1953. I have full confidence that the time will come when a grateful Georgia will officially repatriate him with all the honors he is due as the first democratic leader of the first independent Georgian state in centuries.

---

On 26 May 2011 President Saakashvili bestowed this honorary medal on my sister Nathela, myself, and a select number of Georgians in recognition of outstanding cultural and scientific contributions to the country.

\*\*\*\*\*\*\*\*\*\*\*\*\*\*\*\*\*\*\*\*\*\*\*

237

10040086R00143

Made in the USA
San Bernardino, CA
03 April 2014